WHITE GIRL

WHITE GIRL

A Story of School Desegregation

BY CLARA SILVERSTEIN

The University of Georgia Press
Athens & London

Published by the University of Georgia Press

Athens, Georgia 30602

© 2004 by Clara Silverstein

Set in 10/13 Caledonia

Printed and bound by Maple-Vail

The paper in this book meets the guidelines for permanence
and durability of the Committee on Production Guidelines
for Book Longevity of the Council on Library Resources.

Printed in the United States of America

08 07 06 05 04 C 5 4 3 2 1

Library of Congress Cataloging-in-Publication Data

Silverstein, Clara, 1960–

White girl : a story of school desegregation / By Clara Silverstein.

   p.   cm.

ISBN 0-8203-2662-3 (hardcover : alk. paper)

1. Silverstein, Clara, 1960– —Childhood and youth.   2. White
children—Virginia—Richmond—Biography.   3. Middle school
students—Virginia—Richmond—Biography.   4. Girls—
Virginia—Richmond—Biography.   5. Whites—Virginia—
Richmond—Biography.   6. School integration—Virginia—
Richmond—History—20th century.   7. Ricmond (Va.)—Race
relations.   8. Richmond (Va.)—Biography.   I. Title.

F234.R553S55 2004

975.5'451043'092—dc22   2004007729

British Library Cataloging-in-Publication Data available

In memory of my father, Joseph Lee Silverstein Jr.,
February 11, 1926–March 6, 1968

Contents

Acknowledgments

This story is true to the best of my ability to remember and retell it. I have changed the names and some identifying details of most of the people within it to protect their privacy. For historical background and statistics, I am indebted to *The Color of Their Skin*, Robert A. Pratt's study of desegregation in Richmond (University Press of Virginia, 1992). Also useful for background information was James L. Doherty's self-published *Race and Education in Richmond* (1972). An excerpt from the story was published in *StyleWeekly* newspaper in Richmond on September 11, 2001, to commemorate the thirtieth anniversary of widespread busing in Richmond; another excerpt was published in the online literary journal *Blackbird* in May 2004. Throughout the text, I use the term *black*, rather than *African American*, reflecting the vernacular in use during the time period of the story. The book reflects the careful editing of Jennifer Reichlin and copyeditor Gay Gragson, for which I am grateful.

I am also grateful to those who read and commented on early drafts, especially Fay Chelmow, Theo Collins, Cindy Duffy, Wendy Epstein, Esther Blank Greif, Berkley Lynch, Barbara Rabin, Monica Harari Schnee, Jim Steiker, Joanna Stein, Robin Stein, Michael Toms, Allen C. West, Mary Helen Willett, Michael Paul Williams, Judy Wurtzel, and Sharon Wurtzel.

For their enduring interest and moral support as I kept writing and rewriting this book, I thank Amy Eppler-Epstein, Diana Hume George, Martha Harney, Susan Katcher, Carol Peacock, Bernice Schnee, and Murray Schnee; Boston Herald colleagues Jane Dornbusch and Rosemary Herbert; and my reading group: Kay Cahill Allison, Laurie Burgess, Jody Feinberg, and Judy Gelman. I also thank David Herlihy for his legal advice.

I would not have been able to envision the scope of this book without the guidance of teachers like Ken Ringle, who asked all the right questions at the outset, and Richard Hoffman, who helped me find the essential story to tell. As a writer, I benefited enormously from the advice and direction I received from Mary Jean Irion and workshops at the Writers' Center at Chautauqua, and from Barbara Helfgott Hyett and the Workshop for Publishing Poets.

My family saw me through the long, brooding months of writing and revisions. My mother's assistance with family research was invaluable, as was her encouragement. I am grateful that my husband, George, put up with me while I relived adolescence; he also edited innumerable drafts and steadfastly reminded me to keep the past in perspective. My children, Jordan and Martha, gave me the incentive to retell the past and to look forward to the future.

WHITE GIRL

Prologue. Bedtime Stories

My four-year-old daughter, Martha, pulls the pink comforter up to her chin and asks the same question she asks every night: "Could you tell me a story from when you were little?"

I turn off her reading lamp and snuggle next to her. It is more than five hundred miles from this bedroom to the yellow one in which I slept during my childhood. I picture that room, with its orange and yellow flowered bedspread, oak desk, and window overlooking the dogwood tree in the backyard of our house in Richmond, Virginia. Then I start remembering stories.

I have already told her how I fell off the jungle gym and chipped my tooth, already described roller skating in the street with my dog, Cinderella, at my heels. Tonight, a memory of my seventh-grade history class flashes into my head. I am at my desk, my arm behind a stack of textbooks, surreptitiously holding hands with the boy sitting in front of me. It makes me smile — and cringe. I am white. The boy in front of me is black. I ride a bus to a school where most of the children are black. It is Richmond in 1971. I am supposed to be sitting in class with him. I am not supposed to be touching him.

I can't tell her that story tonight, though. She won't understand. I barely understand a lot of the time that I lived through school desegregation, but I'm going to try. There is no conventional way to relate it — no prince or princess, no magic, no "happily ever after." I became one of the few white children to desegregate a black school because my mother believed in integration, as did my father, who died when I was seven years old. As a child, I was most concerned about succeeding as a student, making friends, and growing up in spite of the court orders sending me from one school to another.

My memory of middle school flares like a match inside a cavern. I see myself creeping around the linoleum corridors, hunched over, afraid someone is going to trip me as I walk by. My white face gleams like a lantern. Everywhere I go, people look. I can't cover myself up.

I have spent twenty-five years trying to seal off this memory, but my daughter's voice has tunneled through. My story is usually lost in the historical accounts of busing. Because I am white, nobody threw rocks at me. No police escorted me to my classroom. I graduated and can still enjoy the privileges that go with being white. But if I learned nothing else, I did come to understand the scourge of racism. I was a minority in school. I was treated with indifference, disdain, and hostility just because of my skin color.

It's not just a slogan for me to "teach tolerance" to Martha and to my seven-year-old son, Jordan. I want both of them to read this story one day and learn that life has not always been one big "multiculti" party on MTV. That positive social change is sometimes forged from hostile faces and cigarette ashes flicked carelessly in the school bathroom. That once upon a time, a preacher named Martin Luther King Jr. had a dream, and my family responded to it.

I still believe in that dream. I just wish there had been an easier way to make it come true.

A school bus looms ahead of me, blocking out the shafts of early sunlight. I hurry my two children along. Today, for the first time, they are taking a bus to elementary school because the building they normally walk to is being renovated. When they peer out the windows at me, I wave.

The sobs come after I turn away. The bright, fall morning blurs. I hurry around a corner to avoid a group of neighborhood mothers who linger, sipping coffee from plastic mugs. They might mistake my tears for anxiety about my children's first day at a new school.

Thirty years before, I ran down Antrim Avenue in Richmond, Virginia, on my way to my first day as a white girl bused into a black school for desegregation. It was 1971, Richmond's first year of widespread busing. I was almost eleven years old, just starting sixth grade.

I remember many other mornings that autumn, when the bus driver waited as I rushed to the stop, late yet again, my stomach threatening to eject the Pop Tart that I had just stuffed down. The whole bus was filled with chatter and cigarette smoke from the other white kids already aboard. I sat near the front with my best friend, Liz, keeping count of the Chevrolet and Plymouth models we liked that year. The morning ride was the easiest part of the day—the numbing drone of the motor, the sway of the seats, the Bonne Bell gloss still shiny on my lips. As soon as I got off the bus, I had to brace myself for a day of being the enemy, a white girl in hostile territory.

Now I pass a group of middle school children milling around on the lawn of a church, waiting for their bus. The girls run their fingers through their hair, tugging their tops down around their emerging hips. The boys cluster under an oak tree, shoving each other and laughing. I walk close enough to smell the fruity shampoo rinsed from their still-damp hair. The scent carries me past their bravado, into the squirmy, self-consciousness of the mornings I spent trying to shower my hair into submission before school. It all comes back in a blinding rush: the misery of being an outcast at school, the despair that I could never fit in no matter what I did, the vague but growing sense that the battle for racial equality was getting lost somewhere in the turmoil of busing.

I walk up the front steps of the home where I now live. It was my choice to move to Boston in 1983, instead of returning to Richmond. I was eager to shed the droopy humidity of Richmond's summer afternoons, the languorous accent, the stifling of my intellectual ambitions behind a pleasant smile. Boston, with its meandering pathways along the Charles River, its elegant Back Bay brownstones, and its gold-domed State House, seemed to have a polish and charm that Richmond lacked. I wanted to pretend that my life had started when I graduated from college, that my Southern past was long ago and insignificant.

I know I never have to go back to that middle school, but dread and shame still flood me. The school bus that pulls away with my children aboard sends me hurtling back into the pain, gloom, and diesel exhaust of the past. I was planning to tell this story like a journalist: court decisions, desegregation orders, racial percentages at each school I attended, test scores and grades to measure my progress and education. That's just the straight line of what happened. The tears that roll out unbidden, after thirty years, etch a more complicated truth.

Joined Hands

When I filled out a high-school questionnaire in 1974, I chose the U.S. Supreme Court's *Brown v. Board of Education* decision as the historic event that most influenced my life. I wasn't even born when the Court called for an end to school segregation, but the decision informed most of my education.

The other event that profoundly affected me was more personal: the death of my father in 1968 due to a heart attack. He kissed me good-bye as I left for second grade one morning and he was gone by the time I came home for lunch. I was seven years old; my sister was ten. My father's death set off a chain reaction that uprooted us from our home, sent us halfway across the country, and put me in the midst of desegregation. It devastated my family life. My mother, bitter and emotionally desiccated in the aftermath of his death, has been a widow ever since. My sister grew up to have no family of her own and to live thousands of miles away. She has asked me to call her Suzanne in this story.

The father I remember was the only dad in the neighborhood who would play "Red Rover" with us. With his bald head towering at least a foot above the tallest kid, he was the most popular member of our team. His long legs and slim build made him look more like a professor than a football player. In our yard, a grassy ten-by-fifteen-foot rectangle replicated in the back of every house on our row, all the kids would chorus, "Red Rover, Red Rover, let Mr. Silverstein come over!" He would grin, lower his head, and run into their line, trying to break through the wall of linked arms. After a few rounds, my father, laughing and out of breath, would say, "I feel like a ping pong ball!" He'd push his glasses back up his nose and say, "Call someone else over!"

We lived in Hyde Park, near the University of Chicago and within walking distance of Lake Michigan. We had no special connection to the city; my father had grown up in Charleston, West Virginia, and my mother in Richmond. Chicago was simply where my father found a job he liked. His specialty was a new area of law at the time—public defender and legal aid programs. *Defense of the Poor*, the book he wrote about public defender programs in each state, had been featured in *Time* magazine. My parents chose our house, in the middle of a long, tan brick row on East 55th Street, because from there he could walk to work at the American Bar Foundation.

When my sister got a new bike and gave me her old one, Dad patiently pushed me up and down the street behind our house, his hand steadying the seat. Try as I might, I just couldn't get the hang of riding. I would wobble one way, then the other, and end up in a tearful heap on the asphalt.

"Keep at it," he said, lifting me up and brushing the dirt off my knees.

When I finally took off in a wobbly circle, he stood by and cheered, "Atta girl!"

In the winter, my father would load the neighborhood kids into his red Chevy and take us ice skating at a makeshift rink—a field that firemen had flooded with hoses. We'd skate from one end to the other until our cheeks turned numb, then troop into a warm-up shed and huddle around a fire behind a wire grate. I still have a photograph of myself ice skating with Shawn, a neighbor boy. We're holding hands and peering into the brutally cold air.

Shawn was black, as were many of our neighbors in Chicago. I frequently played jump rope and bounced Super balls in the street with Sheila, the girl my age who lived next door. Her family was one of the first on our block to get a color TV; I would stand in our yard, peering over the fence, and try to watch through their window. When my parents bought their house in 1962, they chose to live in one of the few racially mixed neighborhoods in the entire United States, a fact that would inform the rest of my life.

When Mrs. Jackson, Shawn's mother, sat in our kitchen and drank tea out of Mom's striped mugs, Mom never let on that she had grown up with Jim Crow laws in Richmond. Mrs. Jackson was a plump five feet tall and had a wonderful laugh that shook her whole body. Their friendly banter drifted out of the kitchen while Shawn, his older brother Charles, my sister, and I played Candyland on the living room rug. We played at the Jacksons' house, too, sometimes piling on the couch under one blanket as we all watched *Bozo the Clown* on TV.

When I started kindergarten at the Ray School in 1965, I often walked to school with my sister and other kids from the neighborhood. At one of the crosswalks, I looked for Charles, who was a student safety guard. He wore a bright orange sash over his coat and importantly waved us across the street. I made up a song, "Someday, I'll Be a Safety Patrol," which I hummed to myself as I walked past him.

I had no idea that it was unusual to go to a public school with black kids like Charles, or that the Ray School was one of the only integrated schools in the entire United States. The civil rights movement was gathering force in the South, hundreds of miles from Chicago. The struggle for black people to vote, sit at lunch counters, and choose any available seat on buses was far removed from our daily lives. In our little corner of Hyde Park, we had already come close to what Rev. Martin Luther King Jr. dreamed about in his 1963 speech at the Lincoln Memorial: "Little black boys and black girls will be able to join hands with little white boys and white girls and walk together as sisters and brothers."

My Father's Last Moments

I wonder what my father was thinking the morning he died. Did he notice any squeezing or burning in his chest as he shaved? Did he continue lathering his face anyway, thinking he could push it away, the way he scraped the stubble away with his blade? He had lived with intermittent chest pain for years, and none of his doctors knew how to treat it. Maybe he felt fine as he came downstairs for a slice of toast and a glass of milk, then put on his hat, buttoned up his coat, and went to work.

Did he kiss me good-bye as I sat at the table, pushing flakes of cereal around in my bowl of milk? I replay and replay that morning, yet his very last minutes with me were so ordinary that I remember none of them.

I walked home from my second-grade class for lunch that day—March 6, 1968—skipping past the slush on the sidewalk, eager to eat my sandwich and chocolate Hostess cupcake with white curlicues of frosting on top. When I arrived at the back door, I saw a swarm of grown-ups in the living room. I thought my mother was giving a luncheon, as she sometimes did for meetings of her Great Books reading group. Mom greeted me with a grim face.

"Go on in the kitchen," she said, and followed right behind me.

"Now, sit down there at the table, next to your sister." I did, wondering if I was in trouble, but still not too concerned.

"Girls," she said. "Your father was having heart chest pains this morning. He called me and asked me to bring him to the hospital. He passed away while we were driving there."

He had just turned forty-two. My mother was forty-one.

I couldn't help but think of Pretty Bird, our pet canary. One summer morning, Mom had found him dead at the bottom of his cage.

Dad lined a cardboard box from Marshall Field with toilet paper and gently lowered the bird's stiff body into it. He closed the lid and set the box out in the front vestibule. The next day, Mom, Dad, my sister, and I trudged down to a vacant lot in our neighborhood. Dad squatted and pulled out some weeds from one edge of the lot. Using a spade, he dug a small hole in the dry dirt. As he placed the box in the ground, he asked us all to talk about our happy memories of Pretty Bird.

"He woke us up every morning with his cheerful singing," said Dad.

"Remember the time he got out and I had to call Aunt Elizabeth to help me get him back into his cage?" said Mom.

Suzanne and I probably each said something like, "I'll miss him."

After we spoke, we each tossed a handful of dirt on top of the box. Dad shoveled more dirt over the hole until it was filled in. We picked clover and daisies to lay on top.

I also remembered Billy, a boy in my class, who was hit by a car. He had been in school on a Friday, and his desk was empty the following Monday. Our teacher announced that he had been struck when he ran out into the street to get a ball. She had tears in her eyes. I stared at Billy's desk, awestruck. How could he be there one day, his blond head and plaid shirt bent over his math exercises, and then never return? The teacher assigned someone else to his desk, so there was no longer an empty spot, but I still felt tearful whenever I thought about it too hard.

I stared at the table now, tracing the white swirls in its yellow Formica with my finger. Then I looked up, first at Mom. Eyes bright with tears, she was struggling to compose herself. Then at my sister, who was shaking her head. Then at the kitchen cabinets, still in the same place where I had seen them that morning.

"You mean," I said, "we won't *ever* see Daddy again?"

Mom nodded, too overcome to speak.

I ran upstairs to my room and shut the door against the murmur of voices and clink of coffee cups in the living room. I looked down at the miniature world I had set up for Pepper, one of my dolls. Just recently, my sister had declared me babyish for still playing with dolls, and I had been slightly embarrassed to play with Pepper ever since. Pepper sat at a table made from a checkerboard on top of a wooden block. A tray of fingernail-sized plastic cups stuffed with cotton "soda" was at her fingertips. Her clothes lay in a pile beside the bed I had made by covering two wooden blocks with a bandanna.

I knelt next to Pepper and tried to put a glass up to her mouth, just like I had the day before, but I couldn't make believe she was drinking. I flopped on my bed and remembered when I had been sick earlier that winter and Dad had held a yellow plastic tub under my head every time I threw up.

"Isn't it wonderful how your body gets rid of whatever is bothering you?" he had said, taking a break from the story he was reading to try and cheer me up. I had smiled weakly.

I heard a tap at the door. I didn't want to talk to anyone.

"Who is it?" I asked.

Aunt Elizabeth came in and hugged me. She smelled of onions. Elizabeth was actually my mother's cousin, and she lived with her husband and teenage son in a walk-up apartment just a few blocks away. She and Mom shared leftovers from our parties, S&H Green Stamps books, and house-cleaning tips.

"I'm so sorry, honey," she said, trying to be nice, but instead squashing me. Mom had called Elizabeth from the hospital emergency room. As Mom waited for Elizabeth to come, an orderly handed her the watch from Dad's wrist and the wallet from his pocket. Elizabeth and her husband, Charles, had driven Mom home.

Elizabeth told me, "Your mom said you don't have to go back to school this afternoon."

I didn't. Instead, I wandered up and down the stairs, in and out of my room, feeling comfortable nowhere. My sister had holed up in her room with the door shut, and I didn't feel like knocking. I peered down the corridor into Mom and Dad's room. The blue spreads that my father's mother, Grandma Bertie, had appliquéd with white snowflakes were neatly smoothed over their side-by-side twin beds. My father's boss, a silver-haired man, was sitting in the bedroom chair, talking quietly with Mom. Leaning against the sill of the window that overlooked the apartments across the street, she didn't even notice me.

In the late afternoon, when most of the company had gone home, Mom came into my room with a plaid suitcase.

"Tomorrow, we're flying to Charleston for the funeral," she said, pulling open my closet door to look at my dresses. My father would be buried in the family plot in his hometown of Charleston, West Virginia.

"Here," Mom said, handing me a green and blue plaid jumper with smocking across the front. "This is dark. People wear dark colors to funerals."

"Can I wear a white shirt with it?" I said.

She nodded. "You'll need pants, tops, socks, underwear," she continued, ticking off items on her fingers.

As she stood watching, I opened my bottom bureau drawer—the one where I used to think a monster lived, until Dad convinced me that it was only imaginary—and began pulling out my Carter's underwear.

"Thursday, Friday, Saturday, Sunday," said Mom. "You'll need four pairs."

Ann and Lee, Mom and Dad

My mother, Ann, never wore black because she called it "an old lady color." Her favorite color was blue, and she wore it almost every day—navy cardigans in the winter; baby-blue, sleeveless blouses and cotton skirts in the summer. She kept her black hair short and parted on the side, her bangs clipped back with a metal bobby pin. The only makeup she ever wore was red lipstick, which she kept in a pocketbook that seemed to have an inexhaustible supply of Kleenex, Bic pens, and Life Savers. Her waist was trim enough for her to tuck in her blouses and cinch her skirts with a belt.

Winter in Chicago was something my mother never could get used to. She had grown up in Richmond, where flowers bloomed in March and snow usually melted the day after it fell. She kept her "shoe boots"—red rubber boots with old loafers inside—out in the front vestibule all winter, grudgingly pulling them on every time it snowed.

"Wooo!" she would say, winding up her plaid muffler and pushing open the front door, "Feel that cold air!" Her voice sounded as deep as the rumble of traffic outside. It was so low, strangers sometimes thought she was a man when she answered the phone.

My mother's education in the segregated schools of Richmond, which she attended in the 1930s and 1940s, had hardly prepared her for the life she lived in Chicago. Yet she had an inquisitive streak that made her want to leave the South to attend the University of Michigan for college and Bank Street College of Education in New York for graduate school. My father also encouraged her liberal tendencies. In Chicago, she taught nursery school every morning at the Hyde Park Neighborhood Club down the street and helped supervise an indoor playground called the Tot Lot. Her classes were as racially mixed as the rest of the neighborhood. Once a week, she and some of her friends took a University of Chicago class called "The Negro in America." They read literature by James Baldwin, Booker T. Washington, and W. E. B. DuBois and discussed Negro history.

In the afternoons, my mother and I sat at the yellow and white Formica-topped kitchen table, a Dr. Seuss book open in front of us. Pointing her index finger at the individual letters, she taught me how to sound out the hiss of the "s," the pop of the "p," and the crunch of the "c" until I could read. The day I haltingly made my way through the first pages of *Hop on Pop* she clapped her hands. When my father came home for dinner, she asked me to read for him, too.

As Mom and Dad, my parents seemed to have a deep and abiding rapport. They met on a student ship in the summer of 1948. My father was on his way to Sweden for an exchange program and my mother was on her way to travel around the European capitals with a girlfriend. Both were taking the summer off from graduate studies in New York — my father, from law school at Columbia; my mother, from Bank Street. As Jews with southern roots, they had an instant bond. The long crossing home gave them a chance to stroll around the ship's deck, watching the water churn past, chatting about what they had seen in Europe and the studies they planned to resume when they returned. Their courtship took place in the bustle of New York's Chinese restaurants, Broadway shows, and Central Park. They married in 1950.

At our house in Chicago, they must have bickered about something, the price of the tulip bulbs he planted or the wrinkles she couldn't seem to iron from the shirts he had to wear to court. But I have a hard time remembering any of their conversations with each other. Anything I try to imagine sounds flat and mundane.

What I do remember is their gestures: his hands brushing her neck to clasp the silver necklace she wore when they went out to the movies; his arm circling her shoulders as we walked across the beach at Lake Michigan. Or the two of them whispering as they passed the binoculars back and forth while we watched the eclipse of the moon in a field near our house. Their togetherness felt as sturdy as the floor under my bed.

After my father died, my mother piled his clothes onto an old couch in the basement, the cleaner's bag covering them like a shroud. She had taken everything out of his closet to give to Goodwill, as if any evidence of his earthly presence was now worthless. She set the tone for mourning: no crying, no complaining. Too much talk about him made her gaze into the distance with a look of great pain, so we mentioned him as little as possible. There were boxes to be packed. As soon as school ended, we would be moving to Richmond.

The day when my mother told us we would be moving probably went something like this: She walked into the living room, her hands pressed together, and cleared her throat. I was annoyed because she interrupted my tea party with my stuffed animals.

Suzanne looked up from the Nancy Drew mystery she was reading on the couch. Long legs that tapered to narrow feet set her up to be much taller than Mom, who was only five feet three. Suzanne pushed back her chestnut bangs and frowned.

"Why do we have to move? What's wrong with it here?" Suzanne said. Her hazel eyes flashed.

Mom looked at her hands, which were so large that she wore men's gloves. "It's not the kind of place I want to bring two girls up alone."

"Why not?" Suzanne challenged.

"Well," said Mom, still studying her hands and the wedding ring that she wears to this day. "If we stay here, I can't give you girls the kind of freedom I think you ought to have."

"What do you mean by that?" Suzanne said. She was already old enough to walk down to Walgreen's drug store with her friends and would soon be ready to ride the commuter train into the Loop to go shopping at Marshall Fields.

Mom hesitated. "A lot of things . . ." she said.

Compared to Chicago, Richmond was a small town. Mom felt safe there among the wide boulevards and red brick houses of her own childhood. Her mother, Grandma Hanna, still lived in Richmond on the first floor of the two-family house in which my mother had grown up. Suzanne and I (her only grandchildren) called her Hanni, as she said the title granny or grandma made her feel too old. Her husband, Grandpa Henry, had died in 1962. If my mother had to raise two children on her own, she wanted to be in a more familiar city, near her mother as well as much of her extended family.

Suzanne said, "Well, I don't want to leave," ran upstairs, and slammed her door.

Mom walked into the kitchen and soon I heard her putting dishes from the drain board back into the cabinets. The soft clink of teacups against the shelves and the thump of the doors shutting sounded vaguely soothing, as if the household was going on as usual. But I wanted more from my mother. I wanted her to gather me up in her arms, let me cry into her cardigan sweater, and tell me everything would be all right. Yet I was afraid of her reaction. Asking her to comfort me might set off the torrent of grief that I sensed she was holding back. Her voice sometimes quavered, but I never saw her crying—perhaps because she didn't want to upset me, perhaps because she feared being unable to cope with the power of her emotions. Her restraint made me feel like I had to conceal my deepest feelings from her, because they would threaten the control she wanted to maintain in herself and in our house.

I stayed in the living room and set a flowered teacup in front of Chang, my stuffed Pekingese dog. Then I gathered him into my arms and put my face into his soft fur. My tears made the fur clump together, but I didn't tell anyone. Chang was all dry the next day and nobody knew that my mother's news upset me, too.

When Martin Luther King Jr. and then Robert F. Kennedy were assassinated in the weeks that followed my father's death in 1968, I watched each funeral on TV. Coretta and Ethel were both widows, just like my mother. Their children had also lost their fathers. Yet these children became famous in their grief. Were they biting their lips and trying to be brave, like I was? Were they embarrassed by the attention? I felt even more alone as I hunkered into a corner of the living room couch to watch, my eyes glazed, my face sullen.

You Talk like a Yankee

On my first day at Mary Munford, my new public elementary school in Richmond, Mom walked me to the front entrance and snapped my photo. The two-story, brick building sprawled across an entire city block. An enormous field—something we didn't have in Chicago, where space around the school was paved over—muffled the sound of traffic whizzing along Cary Street. The windows overlooked a blacktop playground painted with four-square courts and a dodge ball ring. The few trees on the grounds were spindly and gave no shade.

I felt the hot prickle of tears behind my eyelashes. Dad had taken our first-day-of-school photos every year before that. It was September 1968, a few weeks before my eighth birthday. Mom had just taken a job teaching preschool at Grace House, a community center where her class would become as racially mixed as it had been at the Neighborhood Club in Chicago.

The kids in my new third-grade class, who were all white except for one boy, teased me for talking "like a Yankee." I didn't know why this was supposed to be an insult. All I knew about Yankees was the song "Yankee Doodle." I soon discovered that the remnants of the Confederacy cast long shadows through its former capital, even one hundred years after the Civil War had ended. Gray-haired Mrs. Roland flitted around the perimeter of the room like a bird, arms folded behind her back, as she taught Richmond history. She told us that the site for the city was discovered in 1607 by explorers who came up the James River from Jamestown ("the first permanent English settlement in the U.S., older than Plymouth in Massachusetts!" she proclaimed with arm-swinging pride). Richmond became the capital of Virginia in 1780, taking the title away from Williamsburg.

She called the North-South conflict The War Between the States instead of the Civil War. This, I learned, was a southern custom. To call it the Civil War made the Union seem too important. Southerners believed they were fighting for the right of each state to make its own laws. The slaves, she said, were happy in their homespun clothes, singing spirituals as they planted tobacco. She never mentioned that they were the only Richmonders who cheered when the Yankee troops marched into the fallen city in 1865. Nor did she point out the city's former slave market near Fifteenth Street. It wasn't far from a place she made sure to emphasize: St. John's Church, where Patrick Henry, on the eve of the American Revolution, shouted, "Give me liberty or give me death!"

Outside of school, I saw the Confederate flag all around the city: in restaurants, on T-shirts and caps, flying from brick mansions on Cary Street and from trendy row houses in the Fan District. Statues of Confederate heroes lined Monument Avenue, a cobblestoned boulevard that passed within a block of my grandmother Hanna's house. My teacher made us memorize the name of every statue: General J. E. B. Stuart (who rode his bronze horse into eternity right across from the hospital where my mother was born), General Robert E. Lee, and General Thomas J. "Stonewall" Jackson; President Jefferson Davis; and Naval strategist Matthew Fontaine Maury. These were the famous Virginians we learned about, along with seven U.S. presidents born in Virginia, including George Washington. We never heard that soft-shoe legend Bill "Bojangles" Robinson and tennis star Arthur Ashe (whose statue, after tremendous controversy, now graces the western end of Monument Avenue) were also Richmond natives. My mother was the one who identified Arthur Ashe to me as a Richmonder. She added, shaking her head ruefully, that the Country Club of Virginia wouldn't let him play in tournaments on its courts because no blacks were allowed.

Some of my classmates were the descendants of Confederate soldiers, with relics like minié balls, tattered flags, and Confederate dollars on display in their dens. It surprised me to learn that I am a descendant, too. My great-great-grandfather on my father's side, Timothy Harding, fought in a North Carolina regiment. Yet Rebel pride never seemed to interest my grandmother Bertie, who had grown up in the tiny town of Washington, North Carolina. She never petitioned to join the Daughters of the American Confederacy, a group that met to study and glorify the past—not that a Jewish woman would have been accepted at that time, anyway. Maybe her disinterest also came from the years that she had lived in West

Virginia, the region that on the eve of the Civil War separated from Virginia to form a Union state.

In contrast, Bertie's husband, Grandpa Joe Silverstein—a descendant of Lithuanian Jews, not Rebel fighters—adopted the middle name Lee. He chose it while attending Washington & Lee, the college where Robert E. Lee became president after his defeat as Confederate general. Maybe Grandpa Joe simply liked the name, but I suspect he appreciated its power to promote his assimilation as he opened his own law practice in Charleston, married my North Carolina–raised grandmother, and became a city councilor. The name Lee has since been passed down through four generations of my family. It is my son's middle name, to honor my father. I now find it ironic that my son carries this homage to the southern past as he grows up in the heart of Yankee territory.

My grandfather, Henry Wallerstein, was a native Richmonder. Though he had no ancestors in the Confederate army, he had kept a Confederate flag on his desk and Confederate money in his drawer. From what I can tell, he did so out of loyalty to his friends and business associates more than a deep and abiding passion for the old Confederacy. After all, he was willing to marry my grandmother, who had grown up in Mount Vernon, New York. Hanni seemed well adapted to Richmond by the time I knew her, though she still talked like a Yankee. Despite my direct Confederate ancestry and family history, I just couldn't identify with the pride and sadness around me—the idea that the Confederate cause was noble, if doomed. I never felt like this heritage was mine to claim. I had come to Richmond from Chicago with the wrong accent and the wrong sensibilities.

Tomboys

I made friends with other tomboys, who flouted the southern politeness and decorum that I found oppressive. Annemarie Patton had frizzy, blonde hair and thick glasses. She walked to school with her collie, who was named Colonel John Singleton Mosby to honor the leader of a band of Confederate raiders. Colonel used to wait on the football field until recess, when we would come out and let him jump up and joyfully lick our faces. After school, we sometimes played at the Trenches, an old Confederate defense line that looked like a semicircular gouge in a hill of red dirt. A commemorative cannon was mounted at the top of the hill. The Trenches were about a mile from school in a fancy neighborhood named Windsor Farms. The streets, lined with Georgian brick houses, used English names such as Clovelly, Nottingham, Cambridge, and Windsor.

One Saturday, Annemarie and I decided to ride our bikes down one side of the Trenches, then up the other. There were several trails to try. Finally, Annemarie asked, "Are you ready for Dead Man's Trench?"

"What's that?" I said. "Did something awful happen in there?"

"I couldn't say," said Annemarie mysteriously, her voice growing deeper. "It's the steepest one, though."

We wheeled our bikes to the top. The hill seemed to drop almost vertically at that point, but there was a well-worn trail.

I swallowed and asked, "Have you done it before?"

She nodded. "Watch!"

Down she streaked, her hair flying backwards, bike rattling over the pebbles. At the end of the trail, she turned and waved, her glasses glinting.

"Don't be a 'fraidy cat!" she said.

I gulped and pulled the handlebars of my bike into position. Halfway down I tried to brake, skidded, and flew sideways before crashing into bottom of the trench. I came to a halt on my side, my bike on top of my leg, one of its wheels spinning uselessly behind me. I heard Annemarie's footsteps pelting down the trench.

"Clara!" she shouted. "Clara! Are you okay?"

I wriggled my leg and tried to push the bike off me. She lifted the bike and threw it down on the ground beside me.

"You are a sight!" she said, looking somewhat pale behind her freckles. In a quieter voice, she said, "Oh, gosh! I should never have put you up to this!"

I could feel the blood pouring out of my nose. The entire side of my leg was cut where it had scraped along the dirt. I sat up, felt dizzy, and lay back down.

"I'll be okay," I tried to tell her, spitting dirt from my mouth.

"Hold on," she said. "I'll ride home for help."

I nodded, too shaken to protest. I lay back at the bottom of the trench, looking up at the trees overhanging the top of the trail, imagining myself a wounded Confederate soldier, scared and in pain.

Then a voice called out, "Hey! Where's Old Bloody Nose Silverstein?"

Up walked Annemarie's father, carrying a black bag. Annemarie was right behind him.

"You couldn't have found a better person to help you. I'm a doctor," he said, smiling from beneath his graying crew cut. He held a handkerchief against my nose to help stop the bleeding, swabbed my cuts, and even kicked my dented bike fender back into place.

"Good as new!" he said cheerily, pushing the bike as I limped back to his house. By the time my mother came, I was sipping ice water and playing cards with Annemarie. As I left, Annemarie said, "Never go down Dead Man's Trench again!" and I answered, "No way!"

Annemarie and I continued to play together after that bike ride, but I ended up becoming best friends with Liz Harris, who lived a block away. She had straight, auburn hair that fell to the middle of her back and round, blue eyes that made her seem more innocent than she really was. Her build — stocky shoulders and a middle that she called tubby (I thought she exaggerated) — matched her fearless personality. I frequently walked over to play in her basement. Jeans, shirts, and underwear dangled from a clothesline strung across the rafters. On the ironing board, there was a glass Coke bottle fitted with a sprinkler head for dampening the clothes. The whole room smelled like fabric softener. Liz let me try using a sewing machine for the first time, laughing when I ended up with a giant knot in a piece of calico.

Liz and I started meeting almost every day after school, a time I was usually on my own. My mother, busy with her job and errands, usually didn't come home until dinnertime. As an adolescent, Suzanne had developed mysterious interests — she was either out on the clunky, brown bike she nicknamed Rattletrap or in her room with the door shut. She disdained my pastimes as too babyish for her.

As a result, Liz was my best and most available companion. We clipped metal roller skates to the bottoms of our Keds, going up and down the streets until the wheels wore out and the ball bearings scattered. Other days we rode our bikes back to the school playground, digging up the football field in search of the clay that was supposed to be buried under the dirt, or practicing new tricks on the monkey bars outside our classroom windows. It took a blizzard to close the Chicago schools, but in Richmond, a minor dusting could give us an unexpected vacation day. We went "sleigh riding," the southern term for sledding, at the Country Club of Virginia. Our wooden sleds with metal runners rattled down the snow-covered fairways, our teeth banging together, our hats flying off our heads.

For the next several years, our friendship took us through the gravel-lined alleys behind the houses in our neighborhood, under the peeling bark of crape myrtle trees, and into the dank garages that housed broken lawn mowers and antique cars. We chased Wiffle balls past screened porches and concrete patios, tomato patches, and chain-link fences that contained neighborhood dogs. Gradually, the blocks between school, my house, Liz's house, the Exxon station, the apartment buildings across the street, and the Methodist church where our Girl Scout troop met began to feel like home.

Our West End section of Richmond, about four miles from downtown, had been built in the postwar boom of the 1940s and 1950s. Azalea and holly bushes grew around the three- and four-bedroom brick houses, which were separated by sturdy magnolias, oaks, and maples. Family cars were parked at the curbs out front because there were few driveways or garages. Most of our neighbors had middle-income jobs—insurance salesman, postal clerk, gas station owner. One of the streets, Stuart Avenue, was named after a Confederate general.

My house was on Grove Avenue, where four lanes of traffic and the Westhampton 16 city bus line surged outside the front door. A concrete median strip lined with utility poles divided the westbound and eastbound traffic. Our two-story, brick house was set back from the street. There was no fence around the front yard, but we had one pine tree and one oak tree for ornament. There were two apartment buildings across the street, and I could see the young couples who lived there sitting on their balconies eating supper. At the corner was a Baptist church. In the backyard, surrounded by waist-high hedges and a chain-link fence, we sunbathed in lawn chairs or played croquet with cheap, plastic balls.

Inside, our house was dark and musty, with wall-to-wall olive green carpet in the living and dining rooms. Though we all agreed that the carpet was ugly, Mom had been through too much upheaval to even consider redecorating. She placed the Oriental rug from our living room in Chicago on top of the green and red linoleum tiles in the den. The rug didn't reach the edges of the room, leaving about a foot of exposed linoleum all around. She placed our upright piano against one wall, a rickety wooden typing table in the corner, a plant stand under the window, and called it done.

Liz and I sometimes played Monopoly or Sorry at a toddler-sized table in my basement. The room was paneled with pine boards that my sister and I decorated with black-light posters. Everything ended up mildewed.

Our tomboy world insulated me from the prissy girls at school, the ones who still called me "Yankee" and who never forgot to say "Yes, Ma'am" to the teacher. I was far from being a lady-in-training. My knees were always scabbed from spills on my roller skates. My light brown hair jutted out in all directions. I wore shorts under the skirts that I had to wear to school so I could pull off the skirt the minute I started walking home. Though Liz had more of a southern upbringing, she was the youngest in a large family, and her siblings had paved the way for her independence. Our world seemed as filled with potential as the new apartment building going up in the weeds of a lot near the Mary Munford School. One day, we sneaked under the temporary fence after quitting time. From the third story, the smell of fresh sawdust still sharp, we looked out of half-framed windows at the crowns of trees and spires of churches in the distance. In the haze of afternoon humidity, the city beneath us seemed calm and remote.

Freedom of Choice — Yes! Busing — Never!

In the spring of 1970, my fourth grade year, I was playing Monopoly with Annemarie in her basement when I came across a red bumper sticker next to a punching bag. "Freedom of Choice—Yes! Busing—Never!" it read.

"What's this?" I asked.

Annemarie shrugged. "My father put that there."

I told my mother when I got home. I expected her to wave her hand and say, "Oh, it's just something silly."

Instead, she put down the spoon she was using to stir the broccoli boiling on the stove. She wiped her hands on the dish towel and kept her back turned for a minute, her shoulders hunched in her blue cardigan.

"What's Freedom of Choice?" I asked.

"That means people can choose any school they want to. They usually end up choosing the nearest one, so they can walk," she said.

"Like we walk to Mary Munford?" I said.

She nodded, and then turned back to the stove.

"Changes are coming," she said finally. She explained that the city was trying to find a way for black and white children to go to school together, as we had in Chicago.

"What's the big deal?" I said.

"Well, in Chicago, we all lived in the same neighborhood. It's not like that here. Black children and white children usually live too far away from each other to walk to the same schools," she said. "A lot of people don't want things to change here."

Freedom of choice in Richmond was being challenged because of a 1968 Supreme Court decision, *Green v. County School Board of New Kent County*. The court ruled that freedom of choice was not an aggressive enough approach to desegregating the two schools in this rural Virginia county near Richmond. In 1967, despite freedom of choice, only about 115 black children had enrolled in the formerly all-white school; no white children had enrolled in the black school.

In its decision, the court called for a stronger, more forceful, and speedier plan to ensure integration in the two schools.

Spurred by that decision, the NAACP filed a challenge to Richmond's freedom of choice plan. U.S. District Court judge Robert R. Merhige Jr. heard the case, and in the spring of 1970 he ruled that the Richmond School Board had to come up with a plan that would eliminate "racially identifiable" public schools. That year, there were approximately fifty-two thousand students in Richmond's public schools. My elementary school was close to 100 percent white; other schools were close to 100 percent black. Busing was one of the plans for redistributing the racial mix.

The editorial pages of the newspapers, the morning *Richmond Times-Dispatch* and the afternoon *News Leader*, opposed "forced busing." The *News Leader* gathered thirty-seven thousand signatures on a petition opposing the "court-ordered abolition of Freedom of Choice." In the 1950s, the *News Leader* had also supported the massive resistance movement. Through this movement, white politicians led by Senator Harry F. Byrd helped shut down schools in Charlottesville, Norfolk, and other Virginia cities rather than allow desegregation. The segregationists, which included Virginia's governor and attorney general, opposed federal interference in local schools. Integration, they argued, would destroy public education and lead to immoral race mixing. Their sense of honor and cherished way of life was at stake, and they were determined to fight back. It took the federal courts, enforcing the *Brown* decision, to make the schools reopen. The last holdout was Prince Edward County, which managed to keep its public schools closed from 1959 to 1964.

Once Judge Merhige's desegregation ruling was announced, there was a buzz around Mary Munford about who would stay in the school, who would move to the suburbs, and who would try to go to private school. Annemarie told me that as soon as she got into a private school, she would go. The details of Richmond's desegregation plan were still being negotiated, but it was clear that the start of the next school year would bring changes.

When Mom came to pick me up from playing at Annemarie's house a few days later, Annemarie's father met her at the door.

He stood stiffly, his haircut so bristly it looked like he was in the military.

"You're not thinking of trying to find a new school for Clara?" he asked.

"No," she said. "The public schools are fine by me."

"You liberal, you," he teased. Then he added, "Aren't you worried about her education? Those teachers are going for the least common denominator."

"Why not give all kids a fair chance?" Mom said.

"Standards will fall for everyone," he said.

Mom stood in the doorway, jingling her car keys and motioning me to say good-bye.

"I'm going along with it. You have to expect the best, not the worst," she said.

"Model" Schools

One alternative to busing was the John B. Cary experimental school that my cousins, Larry and Phyllis Zeller, helped to start in 1969. Larry, my mother's first cousin, led his household with a booming voice and brusque instructions to his children. Phyllis, who had been his high school sweetheart, had a focus and intensity that belied her small stature. They lived about a mile away from our house, on a side street that looked a lot like Windsor Farms with its Georgian homes. They had a gravel driveway and a tree house in the backyard.

Larry and Phyllis's daughter Naomi was only six months younger than me. She wanted to read all the time. Riding in the back of Larry's blue Chevrolet station wagon, she would bend unperturbed over her book as her younger brother, her sister, and I sang in falsetto. Sammy, two years my junior, and I squirted each other with the hose in the backyard while Naomi read in the beanbag chair in her bedroom. She plowed through *The Hobbit* and other advanced titles that held no appeal to me. At Larry and Phyllis's dinner parties, she sat cross-legged on the sofa and discussed these books, wowing the guests. I learned the word *precocious* from listening to the comments about her.

When Naomi started misbehaving in class at Mary Munford, Larry and Phyllis thought she was bored. In their search for an alternative, they discovered the model school movement. These schools let children direct their own learning outside of a traditional classroom structure. Advanced readers could delve into literary classics; budding scientists could design their own experiments; all students could learn at their own pace and be challenged. There were already a few model schools in operation, including the Lake Normandy School in Maryland.

Phyllis and Larry found several other parents who liked the model idea. They started by asking the Mary Munford principal about launching a model program within the school. When he turned them down, they drafted their own proposal. Phyllis remembers when they approached the superintendent of schools to ask for funding. In one of their first meetings, they told him they wanted the new school to be racially integrated. They were liberal enough to support integration; they also knew of Richmond's pending desegregation lawsuit and didn't want to be accused of running a "white flight" school. Phyllis says the superintendent threw back his head and laughed. "An integrated school?" he roared. "This is Richmond, Virginia!"

Phyllis and her group had the last laugh when their plan was approved by the Richmond School Board. They opened John B. Cary Elementary School in the fall of 1969. As promised, Cary was the most racially integrated elementary school in the city: 60 percent black and 40 percent white, even before busing.

Naomi and Sammy left Mary Munford to enroll at Cary. Naomi's descriptions of her new school made it seem like a giant set from *Zoom*, the then-new creative kids' show on PBS-TV. She and her classmates had discussions of which animal they would rather be — a bird or a whale. They spent half the day on art projects and proudly hung them in the hall. They put on plays for each other. They sat on cushions instead of at desks.

I asked Mom if I could ever go to Cary with my cousins. Larry and Phyllis had wanted her to join their committee from the beginning. But Mom would have none of it.

"Those schools don't do enough with the three R's," she said. "They're too loose. I want you to learn the fundamentals."

"But it's boring to do the three R's all the time," I protested. "Naomi and Sammy get to have fun!"

"School isn't supposed to be fun and games," said Mom. "There's nothing wrong with staying where you are."

My fifth-grade teacher, Miss Wallace, had once taught my mother and, more recently, my sister. Her stooped shoulders accented her crooked teeth. Her southern accent was so thick she sounded like a 45 RPM record being played at 33. Mom and Suzanne both praised her "Art Through the Ages" curriculum, which started with the Greeks and ended with Picasso. She instructed all of us to buy a special notebook. But no sooner had I pasted a sketch of a Greek urn on the first page than Miss Wallace was history herself. In the fall of 1970, there were only about a dozen students in each of the three fifth-grade classes—not enough to justify paying three teachers. This decline in students at Mary Munford reflected a trend around the city. That fall, about five thousand fewer white students enrolled in the public schools than were expected. Black enrollment that year showed much less fluctuation.

The schools had barely opened on time. In mid-August, the school board was still arguing about the best plan to integrate. Finally, Judge Merhige called for an interim busing plan that would be expanded the following year. The faculty was also being reassigned. About two weeks before the start of school, more than eight hundred teachers were moved to other schools in order to provide each school with a racially mixed staff.

One morning, about two weeks after school began, Miss Wallace started class with a quaver in her voice.

"Yesterday afternoon, I learned that I will no longer be your teacher this year. The class is too small. Half of you will go to Mrs. Wilkins's class, and half to Miss Fowler's. And I," her voice broke, "am being asked to retire."

She pulled a Kleenex from her purse and began to wipe her eyes. We were all silent as she read our new class assignments. Annemarie, Liz, and I looked at each other triumphantly when we realized that we would be in the same class.

At the end of class, as I scooped the papers out of my desk, Miss Wallace came over and gave me a hug.

"It's such a sorry shame," she said. "I had really looked forward to teaching you. I just loved having your mother and your sister."

At home, when I told my mother the news, she pressed her lips into a thin line.

"That's not fair to her," she said. "She was loyal to the system. You're really missing out on a good teacher."

Mrs. Wilkins, my new teacher, was black, one of the first to integrate the Mary Munford faculty. The other fifth-grade teacher, Miss Fowler, was also black. Mrs. Wilkins handled our abrupt entry into her class calmly.

"Annemarie, you sit here," she pointed to a desk. "Make yourself a name card so we can all learn your name. Clara, you're over here."

Two black girls, Lenore and Vanessa, were already in Mrs. Wilkins's class. I showed them how to play with Annemarie's dog at recess. All of us laughed at his frantically wagging tail. Vanessa and I were the first to wear pants to school the day after the principal changed the dress code for girls. We grinned at each other as everyone pointed to us all day long.

When I was planning my tenth birthday party, I asked Mom if I could invite Vanessa and Lenore. I wanted to gauge her reaction. I had already played with black children in Chicago, but this situation was new.

"Of course they're welcome," Mom said. Then, she added, joking, "We'll just hope that Mr. Lewis doesn't come after them with a shotgun," referring to an openly racist neighbor.

I invited them, but neither came.

With her hair swept back into a bun and her conservative skirts and blouses, Mrs. Wilkins was the portrait of dignity. She stood at the blackboard and demonstrated handwriting in beautiful, flowing cursive. Our work was checked for neatness as well as quality, and she often pointed out the flaws in my penmanship.

If Mrs. Wilkins was reluctant to discipline the white students, whose parents might retaliate with racial epithets, she didn't show it. From what I remember, although most of the white students were used to seeing black women as "the help" instead of as teachers, they seemed to give her the respect her role required. When I sucked the ink out of my pen until my tongue was covered with green spots, she shook her head in exasperation and said, "Go rinse your mouth out in the drinking fountain." Another time, when Annemarie and I collapsed into giggles because neither of us could pronounce a name in our geography book, she made us stand out in the hall.

Halfway through the year, Annemarie left Mary Munford to go to private school. Her empty desk foreshadowed the departure, over the years, of many other white students who were my classmates and friends. This loss was one consequence of integration that never failed to upset me. When a close friend like Annemarie abandoned the public schools, I felt abandoned, too.

As the weather warmed in the spring of 1971, my class began playing softball against Miss Fowler's class during recess. Mrs. Wilkins paced the asphalt sidelines in her pumps, squinting into the sun, keeping us lined up in the right batting order. Miss Fowler, who was younger, always took a turn at bat. She was dark-skinned, with long legs, and bangs that she combed straight down her forehead.

"Come on, let's go," she said, holding up the bat and then tapping the tip against the dirt of the playing field. Everyone in the outfield moved way back, because she was a power hitter. She'd wobble a bit in her pumps, then swing at the ball. If it was a strike, she sucked in her lower lip, spun around, and tried again. If it was a hit, the ball soared out over the grass, beyond the gloves of the best players in our class. We'd watch it drop as she teetered around the bases, black-framed glasses bouncing on her nose and triumphant grin on her face. I stood at the sidelines, cheering, admiring how she could get all the boys to move back in the outfield, peering up, slapping their gloves expectantly.

Busing Hits Home

The day my mother told me I would be bused to school for sixth grade, she came home from grocery shopping, picked up the *Richmond News Leader* from the porch, and waved it in front of me as I watched *Petticoat Junction* in the living room. It was in the spring of 1971.

"They have the new school districts drawn," she said, pointing to the front page. I snapped off the TV and came into the kitchen, where she had spread the newspaper on the table. Tracing the lines on the map with her forefinger, she said, "That's good for Suzanne!" My sister would stay at Thomas Jefferson High School (usually called TJ). TJ was my mother's alma mater, traditionally all white, and it was considered one of the best high schools in the state. It was within walking distance of our house. Black children would be brought there; my sister would avoid being bused.

My mother peered at the map more closely.

"It looks like you'll be going to Binford. You'll be riding the bus," she added, careful to avoid the more inflammatory, "You're going to be bused." Her face was tight.

"Well, well, well," she said, filling the teakettle, then slipping into her chair. "At least it's settled."

I would be one of the twenty-one thousand children of both races scheduled for busing when school started in the fall. Each school's racial balance was supposed to reflect the entire system: 70 percent black and 30 percent white.

At one time, Binford had been a white school. As Richmond's population shifted, it became mostly black. I would be one of the white children bused to make the school more integrated. It was about three miles from where I lived, in the same general direction as Grandma Hanni's house. If I had driven past the building, I didn't remember it. In fact, I knew nothing about the school. Because it was a black school, no one I knew, neither my sister nor the siblings of my classmates at Mary Munford, had attended Binford middle school.

My attempts to reconstruct my feelings that afternoon come up disappointingly blank. I can remember the sunlight slanting through the window above the sink, the potted plants on the sill, the yellow plastic containers for sugar and flour on the countertop, but I cannot recall one thing that registers on the emotional scale. If anything, I was equivocal, willing to go along with busing because that's what my mother expected and what my father would have wanted. Because of my years in Chicago, integration was normal to me. I was used to being with black people in everyday situations—classes, lunch, kickball games in the street.

The details of Binford—what the cafeteria looked like, how long the bus ride would be, whether I would have any friends in my class-es—preoccupied me more than the idea of going to school with a lot of black people. I had no information from which to imagine my first year at middle school. The journey ahead of me felt like sitting on an airplane flying into a cloud: the view fogged out, leaving nothing but the vaguely sickening motion and the drone of the motor.

I called Liz that afternoon to see if she knew more about our new school.

"We're going to Binford," I said, as soon as she came to the phone.

"Yeah, I heard," she said. "At least it's not Mosby."

Mosby was downtown, in the heart of Richmond's black community. To my knowledge, it had never been a white school. I had heard nothing positive about it, only that it was dangerous, tense, and no place to learn anything. Anyone who lived across the street from me, a district that included Windsor Farms as well as the smaller houses near Mary Munford, was supposed to go to Mosby. Most families seemed to view this school assignment like a low draft number. They were moving or using grandparents' addresses from different school districts, doing everything possible to avoid sending their kids into what they perceived as a war zone.

The governor of Virginia, Linwood Holton, was one remarkable exception, especially because some of his predecessors had supported massive resistance. His children had attended Mary Munford with me, although none of them was in my class. When the busing order was drawn, he sent two of them to Mosby, where each was the only white child in the classroom. He personally escorted his eldest daughter to her first day at the mostly black John F. Kennedy High School; a photo from that day was published in newspapers around the world. In Richmond's *StyleWeekly* magazine in September 2001, younger daughter Anne Holton recalled of Mosby middle school, "It really wasn't going, that first year, to an integrated school. It was going to an African-American school. So in a way, that made it easier. All the white people who were there were . . . really there to be part of the solution."

Many of the children I knew at Mary Munford had a different attitude about staying in the public schools than the Holton family. Their anti-busing arguments probably reflected what they heard at home. One day, Teddy Greene, a know-it-all in my class, stood behind Liz as we lined up to go back into the building after recess. I had disliked him since the day I said I wanted to learn how to play the drums, and he told me, "Girls don't play drums." When I asked why not, he said, "Because they just don't."

"Y'all are crazy, you know that?" he said, looking down on us like a gargoyle. "You're in for it next year."

Liz and I exchanged a glance.

"What do you mean by that?" Liz said, crossing her arms against her chest.

"Y'all are going to get beaten up in that school. You won't last a week. You'd better get out while you can."

The gauntlet was down.

"You're the 'fraidy cat," I said. "You won't even try it."

"I know what's good for me," he said smugly, tossing his hair out of his eyes and blinking at us, like he couldn't believe how stupid we were.

"Yeah, well, too bad you don't know anything," said Liz.

That Friday, Liz invited me to spend the night at her house. I walked over after dinner carrying my extra clothes and toothbrush in a plastic bag. We watched Julia Child's cooking show for a while, taking turns standing next to the TV and mimicking her. Then we pulled out the sofa bed in the basement.

"Are you scared about Binford?" I asked her. "Do you think Teddy is right?"

He had shaken me more than I wanted to admit. Were Liz and I really going to be in danger? I had no reason to think we were, but who knew?

Liz rolled onto her stomach and waved her legs in the air. She gathered her hair into a bunch, then let it drop.

"Not really. Well, maybe. Should we be?"

"I don't want to get beaten up," I said.

"Me neither," she said.

"Well, what are we going to do?" I said.

"I bet it will be fine. A lot of fools just want to make trouble," she said.

"I wish everyone wasn't leaving," I said. "Nobody good will be left."

"We'll have to watch out for each other," said Liz.

We fell asleep watching reruns of *Gilligan's Island*. I woke up in the middle of the night, the room dark, Liz's arm flung across the pillow next to mine. The TV was crackling, showing nothing but black and white fuzz. I was scared about Binford, but I didn't want to tell anyone. It would make me look silly. I wanted to be tough as Mom, looking everyone in the eye and saying, "I don't expect trouble." I got up and switched off the TV, then tossed and turned for the rest of the night.

There was no group like the NAACP to prepare white kids for our new school assignments. The most vocal white parents who didn't oppose busing, the Citizens for Excellent Public Schools, focused on education. They wanted to make sure white children continued to get a quality education in spite of integration. Nobody addressed the day-to-day realities of what it might feel like to be a white child in the racial minority.

National news coverage of mobs outside schools in Little Rock, New Orleans, and other cities had vividly shown some of the horrors that black students faced when trying to integrate white schools. There were also death threats, cross burnings, lost jobs, and other economic retaliation against the black community.

However, as a white child about to be bused into a black school, I did not know what to expect. Few adults encouraged me or other white children to stay in the public schools. While I was trying to do the right thing, I encountered disapproval. Most white people I knew thought children like me were asking for trouble and going somewhere beneath us. We were sure to ruin our education, if we didn't get beaten up first. When I mentioned Binford to grown-ups who politely asked where I would be going to school in the fall, most didn't recognize the name. When I explained that it was a public school, and yes, I would be bused, some looked surprised, while others actually gasped in horror. I was left to duck my head, mumble, and wonder if there was something wrong with me.

Desegregation was a concept that my grandmother Hanni could barely fathom. Comfortable with the established social patterns among her long-term Richmond friends, she seemed to float above the hurly-burly of my life. I remember her as a smiling but distant figure, her white hair combed up from the crown of her head, her plain dresses adorned with pins shaped like flowers. Though she always greeted me pleasantly when I came to visit, she never kept any toys or games in the house for me. After offering me a glass of chilled water and a store-bought cookie or two, she usually sent me off to read a book in one of the back rooms. She never discussed busing with me. It was my mother's job, she thought, to make decisions about my education and child-rearing; she preferred to stand back and carry on with her life as she always had.

Grandma Hanni had lived for nearly forty years in a two-family house around the corner from Stonewall Jackson's statue. My grandfather's youngest brother, Ed, lived in the unit upstairs. The neighborhood, about two miles west of downtown Richmond, was called the Fan District because the streets fanned out from one another. Narrow, two-story brick homes, some connected into row houses, some separated by just a few feet, lined the streets. Most were built in the late 1800s, as Richmond rebuilt and expanded westward after having been burned at the end of the Civil War in 1865. This neighborhood had been overlooked for years as the city grew west and south of the James River, but was just being rediscovered around the time we moved to Richmond. Some of the houses were being restored, their front porches ripped down to make way for bright coats of paint right over their brick exteriors.

My grandmother's parties immersed me in the insular Richmond social order that she and my extended family knew. The maid, Amelia, bustled in and out, setting out cocktail napkins and coasters so the drinks wouldn't sweat on the furniture. Hanni's friends, mostly elderly women who powdered their faces and pronounced my mother's name "A-yunn," stopped by in the afternoons for excruciatingly long visits over glasses of iced tea. There was also a procession of elderly great-aunts and great-uncles: Ethel, with her "special kiss spot" on the back of my neck; Belle, whom everyone called "amazing" because she was ninety years old and still gardened; Clarence, whose eyes swam behind his glasses; Ruth and Morton, who had lived in the same house for fifty years.

"Put on your manners," Mom said before the company arrived. For me, that meant not snacking greedily from the hors d'oeuvres trays, and leaving the best seats on the sofa for the grown-ups. For my mother and grandmother, it meant an elaborate series of southern hostess phrases and gestures. With the arrival of the first guest, they started reciting their scripts: "So nice to see you, so glad you could come, let me get you a drink, isn't it hot today." Many of the guests brought little gifts like cocktail napkins or homemade cookies, which my grandmother accepted with a hearty, "Aren't you nice!" Departing guests set off a whole new round of pleasantries: "Do come again, please send me that recipe, you're a dear."

I had trouble understanding the Virginia accent—*water* sounded like "waw-tuh," *out* like "oat." The whole scene seemed like it was happening on stage, remote from my seat on a bench in the entry hall. During these parties, I wondered what happened to the mother I knew—the one who calmly told Annemarie's father she expected the best from the public schools, but also the one whose shoulders sagged as she sipped her afternoon glass of iced tea. She recited her hostess lines with a smile, but I knew how much determination as well as sadness she hid behind it.

Many of the visitors had been family friends since my great-grandparents moved to Richmond in the 1880s. Both my great-grandparents' families came from the same small village near Ulm in southern Germany. They were part of the early wave of German Jews to settle in Richmond.

The city's most prominent gentile families called themselves FFVs—First Families of Virginia. Some could proudly trace their roots to the Jamestown Colony. Most were Episcopalian. Jews weren't invited to their parties or their social clubs and weren't allowed to buy houses in fancy neighborhoods like Windsor Farms. My great-grandparents joined the Beth Ahabah synagogue and the

Lakeside Country Club, the only club in the city that would admit Jews. The Country Club of Virginia, which would not allow Arthur Ashe to compete in tournaments on its courts, made it clear that Jews were also barred when my great-uncle married for the second time. His Episcopalian wife was already a member. The club let her retain her individual membership, but because my great-uncle was Jewish, they refused to let him join. He was allowed to come as her guest only. I wonder why she didn't resign right away. Most of my family's friends were Jewish, the owners of jewelry shops, grocery stores, and other small businesses. Around 1968, when I moved to Richmond, there were about 8,000 Jews in greater Richmond's population of 550,000—less than 1 percent. This gave me quite a different experience than someone growing up in New York or another city with a large Jewish population.

My family were Reform Jews, which meant we didn't keep the traditions that an Orthodox Jew would. We never celebrated the Jewish Sabbath on Friday nights. None of us kept kosher. There was one delicatessen in Richmond, but we hardly ever went there because my mother and grandmother disdained the clientele as "that deli crowd." Their attitude reflected an old division in the American Jewish community. The German Jews generally emigrated from Europe earlier, giving them more time to accumulate wealth and become assimilated into the United States. They looked down on the Eastern European immigrants, who generally came later, bringing Old World sensibilities and few assets. Perhaps because of this, I never even saw lox and bagels, chopped liver, knishes, or other typical Jewish foods until I was a teenager.

We lit the Chanukah lights each December, but we also celebrated Christmas, decorating a small tree in the dining room and exchanging presents Christmas morning. Many Jewish families in Richmond did. Some even threw their own holiday open houses, complete with eggnog and Smithfield ham biscuits. Mom grew up going to many of these parties. It was the southern Jewish way to assimilate. With my light brown hair and blue eyes, I was sometimes told that I didn't "look" Jewish. My response—to feel lucky—fit right into the popular thinking at the time. Visible ethnic differences were something to downplay. If I could easily pass as a gentile, it was to my advantage. Never mind that the popular distaste for Jewish looks was misguided in the first place. I grudgingly sat through religious school each Sunday morning at Beth Ahabah. I hated getting up early and squeezing into my patent-leather shoes instead of lacing up my sneakers. My teachers seemed more interested in Joseph's coat of many colors and other ancient Biblical tales than in anything more recent, such as politics in Israel. Sometimes, I felt the majesty of God's voice vibrating through the organ pipes in the sanctuary when I recited the *sh'ma*, the Hebrew prayer expressing a bond between "The Lord Our God" and the people of Israel. I imagined a giant, shadowy face on the sanctuary's ceiling, peering down at me. It was awe-inspiring but short-lived. I basically felt alone, without earthly or heavenly guidance.

I remember only about a dozen other Jewish children at my elementary school. We sang Christmas carols in music class and decorated construction paper eggs during Easter—and never thought to protest. We didn't want to call attention to ourselves for being different.

Yet there was no escape the day in the cafeteria that a classmate turned toward me and said in a loud voice, "The Jews killed Jesus, you know." I remember nothing that might have provoked him; he was probably just repeating something he had heard on the playground, gauging its impact.

Everyone fell silent, waiting for me to react. My mouth went dry around the bite of bologna sandwich I was chewing.

"Yeah, well?" I said. I had no idea what he was talking about, but his accusation put me on the defensive.

"So you're a Jesus-killer."

"No, I'm not," I said.

"All Jews are," he said.

"Just shut up. I've never killed anyone," I said.

Liz jumped in, "Yeah, shut up, you retard!"

He did shut up, but I could barely eat another bite of my sandwich after that. What had I ever done to him? Or to Jesus, for that matter?

I learned about the Holocaust by chance, when my fourth-grade teacher saw a swastika drawn on the knapsack of one of the boys in the class. She called him up to the front of the room.

"Go home and wash out that awful thing," she thundered, as the rest of the class listened. "It belonged to Hitler, and he killed millions of Jews."

I now wonder why my religious school teachers never taught me about the Holocaust. Maybe they considered the subject too unpleasant for children. Maybe my family, so proud of their heritage that they used to recite part of the Passover seder in German, couldn't bring themselves to admit the horrors of Nazism. They were already safely in the United States when Hitler rose to power. Maybe the silence also helped the Jews in Richmond protect themselves. They had been able to prosper and find a place for themselves, not as exalted and as privileged a place as that of non-Jews, but still comfortable. To dwell on the Nazi horrors threatened what status they had gained, made them realize that they could be sent away on the whim of someone more powerful.

Jim Crow's Legacy

My grandmother's friends called the black women they hired for domestic duties "the help," and they all seemed to employ at least one "girl" for their housework. Hanni used a day worker named Amelia. Following the southern custom, Amelia was always addressed by her first name, but she always called my grandmother "Miz Wallerstein." She called me "Miz Clara" because I was a child. On the days that Amelia came to work, she changed from her street clothes in a small room at the back of Hanni's house. Into a closet went her pocketbook and off came the pumps and sheath dress that she wore to ride the city bus to work. Over her bony frame and gray-streaked hair flattened by clips went a gray dress with a white collar and well-worn loafers. She had worked for the family for years. The first day she saw me after we arrived from Chicago, she gave me a big hug, clamping me to her uniform, which smelled like Ajax. In a certain way, she was like family—part of a long, southern tradition of relationships between white and black people that were often more like *Driving Miss Daisy* than *Gone with the Wind*.

There had been a succession of other maids before Amelia. Some worked exclusively for my grandparents; others split their time between my grandparents, Ed, and other members of the extended family. We still have photos of some of these women, taken on the front porch. They slicked the kink from their hair, pinned it into tidy buns. They wore white aprons over their uniforms. Were they embarrassed to go out front to pose for these pictures, away from the back doors and kitchens that were their usual province? We also have recipes from a few of the maids, written in Hanni's flowing script. How ironic that these women didn't know how to write down their recipes, and that my grandmother never really learned how to cook. Hanni collected recipes from all her friends, probably because recipe swapping was expected of southern women, but all I ever saw her do was toast bread and boil frozen vegetables.

When my mother was little, the maids lived at the house. In a way, they formed a buffer between my mother and her parents. They disciplined but also nurtured, as they fed my mother "Cho-Cho the Health Clown" sandwiches, watched her wheel up and down the street on her bicycle, and met her at the front door when she came home from school. One maid, Lucille, let my mother sit on the back porch after school as Lucille played the numbers with the runners who went from house to house, or waited for her boyfriend to stop by for a brief, somewhat clandestine, visit. My mother later said she felt privileged getting an insider's glimpse into a black person's real life.

Black men had service jobs, too, usually as gardeners or chauffeurs. A few were caddies at the Lakeside Country Club, where my grandfather was a golf champion. Apparently, my grandfather was so well liked that a group of caddies came to pay their respects at his funeral, even though they had to sit in the back of the synagogue.

My mother did her own cooking and laundry but hired maids to come once a week to clean the house. I remember Alberta, a light-skinned black woman with long arms and legs, from Chicago. When I was about five, I sat at the kitchen table watching her sweep the floor. Her wrinkled face looked like an old walnut shell. My mother was upstairs resting in her bedroom and Suzanne was outside riding her bike up and down the street.

"Black skin is ugly," I said.

Alberta stopped sweeping and frowned at me.

"Sit down," she said, motioning me into a chair at the kitchen set. She propped the broom against the wall and sat down next to me.

"Now, hold out your hand."

She found a piece of white notepaper and held it up against my wrist. Then she held her own wrist next to the base of the lamp at the table.

"See, now, your skin is white, like this piece of paper." I stared at it, thinking that no, my skin was really more of a peach color, not stark white like the paper. But I kept listening.

"And mine is brown like the lamp here. But all skin is the same. Feel it," she said. Gingerly, I poked my index finger at her gnarled brown knuckles. "Now, close your eyes. Does it feel any different than yours?" I had to admit that it felt rough, but I would never guess its color unless I opened my eyes.

"OK," I said, and stopped the conversation by getting up, opening our cupboard, and pulling out a Fig Newton. I felt humiliated. I had said something far worse than I had intended.

I was too ashamed to tell Mom at the time, and Alberta kept right on working for us. When I finally recounted this conversation to my mother some twenty years later, she asked, "What made you say such a thing?"

"I don't know," I said, and I still don't. It was probably something as childish as not liking curly hair.

"Good for Alberta," said Mom, her eyes looking past me as she remembered this tall, proud woman. "It took a lot of dignity for her to say that."

The civil rights movement, with its freedom marches, voter registration drives, and sit-ins at lunch counters, didn't touch my early life in Chicago or Richmond. The closest I came to it was watching a PBS special about civil rights with David, one of my Silverstein cousins. While we were lying on the carpet of my aunt Betty's bedroom, we saw fire hoses knocking down a line of black people. Dogs snarled at them and a policeman with a bullhorn ordered, "Move on back. Move on back."

"How can water knock them down?" I remember asking David, already a teenager and old enough, I thought, to know everything. The rest of the conversation probably went like this:

"Fire hoses are really powerful," David answered.

"Why are they being knocked down?"

"The police don't like what they're doing."

"What are they doing?"

"They want to vote and sit at lunch counters where white people are allowed to sit."

"That's all?" I asked, incredulous. "For that, they're being knocked down?"

I had never seen civil rights marches, police dogs, and fire hoses in Richmond. Virginia had a more polite veneer. The myth was that everyone got along, as long as they knew their place and stayed in it. Political maneuvering, like massive resistance (shutting down schools around the state rather than allowing integration), was the preferred method of protesting. Removing stools from the lunch counters in downtown drugstores and benches from the lawn at the State Capitol was another tactic. It kept people from facing the dilemma of where to sit.

"People felt more comfortable standing up to be integrated," my mother used to joke.

By the time I moved to Richmond in 1968, the "Colored Only" and "White Only" signs from the Jim Crow era had been removed. I saw vestiges at the Byrd movie theater, which had a separate balcony where the colored people used to sit and a water fountain on each side of the lobby. Some of the downtown stores had completely shut down their lunch counters, leaving the empty juice dispensers and gleaming swathes of Formica as a ghostly reminder of the city's resistance to change.

The Richmond public schools, though no longer segregated by law in 1968, looked a lot like they had when my mother started Richmond Normal School in 1933. Everyone in her class was white because that was the law. She and her classmates sang "Dixie" at assemblies and were given a day off for "Lee-Jackson Day," which celebrated the birthdays of Confederate generals Robert E. Lee and Stonewall Jackson. The only black adults allowed in the school were janitors, lunchroom workers, and maids picking up kids after school.

The city's Coloreds, as they were called then, went to Colored-only schools. These schools were given furniture and textbooks that had already been used by the all-white schools. Thomas Jefferson High School, from which my mother graduated in 1943, had tennis courts, a track, a football field, a baseball diamond, and a planetarium. Colored high schools made do with multipurpose rooms for lunch, assemblies, and gym. The black teachers in these schools (white teachers never worked in these schools, and black teachers never taught white students) were paid less than the white teachers at white Richmond public schools.

Right after the *Brown* case was decided in 1954, an editorial in the *Richmond News Leader* summed up the reaction of many white Richmonders: "This newspaper, as its readers know, believes in segregated schools. We also believe in abiding by the law. . . . But the court should not misunderstand or underestimate the depth of resentment this opinion will create among a people who feel they have been wrongly imposed upon."

Richmond didn't close its schools during the massive resistance movement. Leading the fight against closing the schools was Lewis F. Powell Jr., chairman of the Richmond School Board at that time, and later a Supreme Court justice. Though he expressed his support for public education, he also said he thought that the extent of integration could be minimized. Instead, in a classic technique of gentlemanly resistance, officials decided not to use any school buses whatsoever. Students were expected to find their own way to school. Most kids walked to whichever school was closest. And because the city's neighborhoods were racially segregated, the schools essentially stayed segregated. Another form of resistance was a Pupil Placement Board, established by the state in 1956 to assign students to schools in each locality. Any student could apply to any school. But the board seldom deemed black children eligible to attend white schools in Richmond or elsewhere. The board disbanded in 1966, the same year that Richmond's freedom of choice plan went into effect.

Richmond's freedom of choice plan gave parents the freedom to choose any school in the city, as long as space was available. This sounded good in theory, but the school board was often slow about placing black students in white schools. Once a black child made the switch, the child was not allowed to go back to a black school. On a practical level, it was inconvenient for black parents to transport their children to schools that were sometimes several miles from the neighborhoods where they lived.

It must have taken a lot of determination for Phil Robinson, the black boy in my third-grade class, to get into Mary Munford. There were a few other black kids who made it into Mary Munford, but generally not more than one per class. Phil intelligently answered questions in class, drew beautiful still-life pictures in art class, and generally seemed to fit in during the school day. I don't remember anyone calling him "nigger," though it probably happened. I doubt the other boys invited him to their birthday parties or their weekend excursions to Virginia Beach. When it came to socializing, he lived behind what W. E. B. DuBois labeled "the veil," where black and white people could see each other but not interact as social equals.

The other black people I knew in Richmond at that time also lived behind this veil, woven from as many social conventions and polite phrases as my mother and grandmother recited at their afternoon cocktail parties. In Chicago, my family and I had lived outside the veil, interacting with the black people we knew as neighbors, not as representatives of their proscribed social roles. When I moved to Richmond, the veil immediately dropped into place. As a child, I wondered why it was there, but didn't have any power to lift it.

Liberal Teacher, Southern Lady

At her job at the Grace House community center, my mother was "Miz Ann," the teacher for black kids, white kids, and a Vietnamese brother and sister whose parents were refugees from the war. Most came from low-income families, though the NAACP lawyer who eventually became the mayor of Richmond and a state senator sent his children there for a session or two. A college dropout with shoulder-length brown hair drove the bus that brought the kids to and from school each day. There were also long-haired VISTA volunteers, who had signed up to work in a program like Grace House so they wouldn't have to fight in Vietnam. They wore peace signs around their necks and T-shirts that said, "Bread, Not Bombs."

The summer I was eight years old, I went every day with my mother to the preschool, where I pounded Play-Doh and worked puzzles with the children. Together, we watched the pet gerbils race around their cage on a table in the corner of the classroom. At outdoor play time, I set the kids up on Big Wheels and tricycles in the pea-gravel-lined backyard. When it didn't rain, I helped serve sandwiches and pour milk at wooden picnic tables.

My mother seemed comfortable as the kids clamored around her. She paced the classroom in her below-the-knee skirts and tan Hush Puppies, setting up blocks, leading "This Old Man" and other songs in her alto voice, and serving lunch. As a preschool teacher, my mother followed in Hanni's footsteps. My grandmother started her career as a pianist and music teacher in the 1930s because the family needed extra money. She eventually became the owner and director of the Tuckahoe Nursery School, known informally as "Miz Wallerstein's School."

Richmond's FFVs and other elite families had somehow chosen my grandmother's humble school, a converted white clapboard house in suburban Henrico County where children baked cupcakes and pushed scooters up and down a hill in the backyard, as a worthy place to begin their children's education. People used to joke that the school was "St. Wallerstein's" because so many of the children ended up going on to one of Richmond's private Episcopal high schools, St. Catherine's or St. Christopher's.

My mother had the chance to take over Grandma Hanni's school, a successful business that had the potential to give her an income for dozens of years. Her choice of Grace House shows both the depth of her social commitment and her desire to rebel. She had left Richmond at age seventeen, an academically ambitious and socially acceptable graduate of the city's segregated schools. She came back a young widow with a social conscience that she was willing to act on — though only up to a point.

In a way, my mother lived a double life. Her job was one compartment of her life; her connection to the habits and customs of her Richmond upbringing another. Some days, she read a book by the swimming pool at the Lakeside Country Club, where Jews could be members but blacks were excluded. On other days, she and my grandmother entertained, handing out bourbon on the rocks from a bar set up at a card table. They graciously thanked everyone for coming, while the maid picked up the dirty napkins and washed the glasses. My mother was as comfortable in this world as she was at the head of an integrated classroom.

My mother may have been able to handle her dual roles, but I sometimes fell into the confusing gap between the two. The summer I helped Mom at her job, I played pool in the room behind the front offices as she went to meetings or cleaned up the classroom. A few older kids hung out there, waiting for the community center's afternoon program for teens to begin. I joked a lot with Doug, an eleven-year-old black boy who always dressed tidily in a polo shirt and chinos, even on the hottest summer days. He patiently taught me how to bank my balls off the sides of the pool table. When I once jabbed the ball so hard it flew off the table, he laughed and said, "Dang! You're going to hit a home run that way!" My face reddened, but I laughed, too.

One day, Doug and I both accompanied my mother and the preschoolers on a field trip to the public swimming pool at Brook Field. The park was in a black neighborhood on Richmond's North Side. It was here that Arthur Ashe had learned to play tennis. When we arrived at the park, I herded the three-year-old girls into the women's changing room. To my surprise, most of them were planning to swim in their underwear.

I whispered to my mother, "Why don't they have any bathing suits?"

"They can't afford them," she whispered back. "Some of them have never been to a pool before."

I went out and dipped my toe into the kiddie pool, deciding whether to stay and help with Mom's class or venture into the big pool, where I could swim.

My mother saw me hesitating and said, "Go ahead and swim over there. The rest of us will be here, so just come on back when you're ready."

I looked for Doug. He wasn't in the wading pool. He had melted into the crowd of laughing, splashing black people in the large pool. I envied his blackness. I was used to being in a mixed crowd, but here I was the only white person in the entire adult pool—pale, conspicuous, exposed in my flowered tank suit.

I walked over to the big pool, feet and face burning in the midday heat. As I passed the other people at the pool, their towels laid out on the concrete, a hush descended. I wanted to hide under one of the towels to avoid their eyes.

Doug climbed halfway up the ladder and waved to me. Relieved, I walked over and jumped in. He splashed water into my face and I tried to dunk him, laughing. Heads turned. Not only was I the only white girl in the pool, I was also obviously friends with a black boy. Nervously, I kicked and splashed, not wanting to put my feet down and feel trapped.

"Let's go off the diving board," I said.

More heads turned as I followed Doug out of the pool. I walked to the end of the board and tried to do a cannonball. I was so nervous, I let go of my knees halfway through the jump, and my body hit the water with a loud smack. I was relieved to be under the surface, if only for a second or two, before I had to swim up and face the stares again.

When I did surface, my skin stung and Doug was laughing

good-naturedly at me. In another situation, I probably would have laughed at my belly flop, too. But here, I felt too embarrassed.

"I'm going back to my mom," I told Doug, and passed back through the crowd with my head down, my shame silencing me as I took my place, handing out towels as the kids lined up.

The Buses Roll

I remember my mother walking me to the bus stop—August 30, 1971, the first day of busing in Richmond, a few weeks before my eleventh birthday. I was glad that she had made special arrangements to go into work late, but I was embarrassed, too.

I tried to talk her out of walking with me as I ate a bowl of cottage cheese for breakfast.

"C'mon, Mom," I said. "You can go to work. Don't worry about me. I'll be fine."

"No, I want to walk with you," she said, taking a sip of her tea with milk. "I want to get you off to a good start."

"Oh, really!" I said. "I'm not a baby."

"Just let me this once. I want to. It's your first day of middle school and all."

Beneath the table, our dog, Cinderella, thumped her tail. She waited under the table every morning, hoping that we might drop a crumb for her to lick up.

"Here, Cindy," I called, using her nickname. She skittered across the linoleum and jumped up into my lap, scratching my bare legs with her toenails. I hugged her and patted her head. Half poodle and half terrier, her black fur stuck together in clumps all down her back. She had white eyebrows, a white chin, and white paws.

"She doesn't have to ride the bus," said Mom with a smile. "She's already integrated."

We both laughed.

"All right, all right, let's go," I said, gathering up my blue, loose-leaf notebook and my handbag.

We walked together, our feet scuffing the sidewalk, pale sunlight sifting down through the crape myrtle trees that lined the street. In an hour or two it would be hot enough for my sleeveless blouse to stick to my back, but right now it was cool and the asphalt street was still slightly damp from the dew.

"Hurry up," said Mom, as I trailed behind her. "You don't want to miss the bus."

"Mom, I'll be fine," I said.

She nodded, and we continued walking in silence. Maybe she was worried that people would be carrying "No Busing" signs and yelling at us when we reached the bus stop, but nobody was. The rush hour traffic whizzed along Patterson Avenue, the drivers oblivious. We were just a group of kids milling around at the corner. When the bus pulled away, Mom waved to me through the window.

That was the only day she ever walked me to the bus. It was her way of telling me that she wanted me to go to this school, that she'd help me face any protestors who showed up that day. Maybe my father would have helped bring the lawsuits that led to desegregation in the first place, and then he would have proudly escorted me into the school. Maybe he would have sat beside me on the living room couch at the end of the day, patiently reading the newspaper or playing cards with me until I was ready to tell him how strange it all felt. I had no doubt that he wanted me to go to a school like this, but now it was up to my mother to see me through it.

Nobody was outside yelling or waving posters when my bus pulled up to Binford's main entrance on Floyd Avenue. There were about 650 students at Binford. The racial percentages, the subject of so much debate, were right within the range set by Judge Merhige: 70 percent black and 30 percent white.

The gray bricks of the school building rose three stories. It looked like a medieval castle. It had a granite arch over the front entrance, second-story bay windows with beveled glass panes, and Gothic letters announcing "Binford School." I walked up the granite stairs and into the assembly hall, where the entire school convened. From the podium on the stage, Mr. Harper, the white principal whose no-nonsense voice matched his iron-colored hair, boomed forth instructions for us to be orderly.

I peered back into the auditorium and saw row after row of black faces. I didn't recognize any of them. I shivered with the strangeness of the whole situation. I looked down and fidgeted with the handbag my grandmother had given me. It was made of cloth woven with signs of the Zodiac. I rubbed my hand across Virgo, then Libra. I was born on their cusp. What would my horoscope predict about this day, this year? Before I could think much about it, I had to stand up and find Mrs. Gregg's classroom, which would be my homeroom.

I sat next to Sandra, a white girl I recognized from Miss Fowler's class at Mary Munford. She kept her face hidden by thick glasses and long, black hair, and usually said little. I recognized a few other people from Mary Munford. Everyone else was a stranger.

The plump, elderly Mrs. Gregg was stumped when she first called roll. She had been reassigned to Binford from an all-white school where children answered to names like Virginia, Lewis, or John. "Shar-o-lynn," she said carefully. "Zo-bia. Flor-net-ta. Ty-rone. Reg-i-nald." The bell rang, and it was time for first period.

On the south side of the building, concrete ramps, all painted maroon, led from one floor to another. Staircases went up and down the north side.

"Up the ramps, down the stairs," called the seventh-grade monitors stationed throughout the halls, reminding us of the traffic flow. I carried a copy of my schedule on top of my notebook as I traipsed from one floor to another in search of a different classroom for each subject: math, science, French, orchestra, gym, social studies, and English.

In the hall, after the assembly, my white skin seemed pale and conspicuous in the throng of black people. I felt everyone staring as I passed by. I kept my eyes on my schedule. I said nothing when a black boy bumped into me so hard I nearly dropped my books and another held out his foot to try to trip me. The monitors, who were black, appeared not to notice. I didn't want to cause trouble. I saw Vanessa, the black girl who had been in my class at Mary Munford, walking down the hall with a noisy group of black girls.

"Hi!" I shouted and waved. She shot me a withering look, as if to say, "So long, white girl." Then she walked on with her friends. I cringed and kept walking.

No One Wants You Here

The first few months of middle school I remember in a physical way: I kept my head down, body stiff, and shoulders hunched forward so I wouldn't have to look at anyone. To be friendly was to invite a reaction like Vanessa's. Every time I walked through the halls, which was at least seven times per day between switching classes and going to the cafeteria for lunch, the glares, elbows in my side, and occasional outstretched foot trying to trip me reminded me that I was perceived as an invader. Trained from an early age to be racially open and to accept integration, I was stunned by the hostility.

The memories come back in a collage: I remember the girls' bathroom, a crowd in front of the mirror, their elbows jostling me so I can't see my own face. Their combs lift their hair high, higher, into proud aureoles. My own hair is lying flat against my scalp, limp along my shoulders. The tap of a pack of Kool cigarettes against the wall. Mentholated smoke blurring the air. The sting of hot ashes flicked onto my bare arm.

I back up. Don't say anything. Slip into a bathroom stall, lock the door, and rattle it to check if the lock really works. Just a flimsy metal bar against the possibility that a girl could open the door to the bathroom stall and stare at me on the toilet, her rude laughter echoing through the room. It has already happened once, could happen anytime.

I pee fast, the hot, shameful gush of it. Wipe fast. Twist the faucet at the sink in the corner, where a few wiry hairs from one of the girls who fixed her hair before me have fallen into the white bowl. Don't even try to get a paper towel, because the crowd swirls around the dispenser. I might have to say, "Excuse me," and bring on hooting laughter. Rush out, breathless, stand against the wall for a minute, holding my books, remembering where I have to go for my next class.

Other memories come from the girls' locker room in the school basement, across the hall from the cafeteria. Loretta, the only other white girl in the class, and I are in a corner, cowering, as we change into our baggy, yellow gym suits with snaps up the front. All the other girls are staring at us. I'm too pudgy in the middle, too big on top, too pale everywhere. Upstairs in the gym, calisthenics. I'm the last picked for any sport. A volleyball game, an accidental collision, an angry shove to the floor. The teacher blowing her whistle, motioning me to get up. Loretta, the other white girl, with her palms up—she can't help me. I limp back into position, avoid the ball then and forever. No showers. Deodorant sprayed at my sweat. Disheveled for the rest of the day.

In the cafeteria, someone hawking up phlegm behind me. The warm spittle oozing into my scalp. The boy and his friend running past the metal shelves where lunch trays slide, laughing, "Aww, haw, haw." Two white girls handing me a napkin, marching me into the bathroom, "Wipe it up." My scalp prickling as if it had been slapped. No point in telling a teacher—what am I, a crybaby? The teachers try to pretend this is an ordinary school, and they never use the words *black* and *white* to describe us. They are stuck working here, and they don't appear to know the first thing about helping us get along.

Shut up and put up. No one wants you complaining. No one wants you here at all.

Black Is Beautiful

As a white person, I was automatically in the out crowd at Binford. The coolest kids in the school were black. They wore metal spoons hammered into bracelets and carried plastic Afro picks or metal "cake-cutters" in their back pockets, the handles wiggling as they jive-walked the school's linoleum corridors. They confidently sang phrases from the Temptations or the Jackson Five in a falsetto that echoed through the halls. At recess, they cranked up their transistor radios in the corner of the playground and danced. The dancing was nothing like the *American Bandstand* show I had seen on TV, in which white teens wiggled their hips at each other. The kids at Binford bent their knees and shook their backsides. Another dance step was the "clacker," a sideways jump that brought their feet together in midair.

After watching them enviously, I decided that I needed to improve my own dancing. One Saturday, I bought a Sly and the Family Stone 45 RPM at Gary's record store at the Willow Lawn Shopping Center. When I got home, I went down to our basement and turned on the yellow plastic record player, a gift from my mother's great-uncle Clarence. As the music blared, I leaned forward and tried to imitate what I had seen. I felt too foolish to tell even Liz about this project.

I practiced the following week after school, jumping sideways enough times to learn the clacker. When I did it at the bus stop, one of the seventh graders who waited there pointed and laughed at me. I was embarrassed. How could I show anyone what I had learned when our school didn't even have dances? If I asked the black kids for help, I thought they'd laugh at me, too. It wasn't my dance to claim. I stopped trying to learn.

The black girls playfully shoved each other as they stowed their belongings in the coatroom. I had finally figured out how to understand the white southerners. Now I had to get used to the way these girls talked, the accent and slang unfamiliar to me.

"Who you go with, girl?" one girl asked another, pointing to the initials she had penned on the back of her spiral notebook.

"Aww, haww, haww," answered the first girl. "Ain't none of your bid-ness."

Another girl scrawled "Tootsie" on the back of all her spiral notebooks, making the O's like upside-down hearts. "Tootsie + S.O.V.S.," she wrote. It took me a while to figure out that Tootsie was her nickname, and S.O.V.S. was "some one very special."

Many of the black kids used nicknames that had nothing to do with their real names. Nobody ever told me the reason for this, though it could date back to slavery days, when black people wanted to name themselves instead of using the names that the owner gave them. At school, nicknames ricocheted around me without explanation. By listening carefully, I eventually learned to identify "Tiny," "Li'l Sis," and "Tiger." I made up a nickname for myself: Quicksilver. I wanted a name that endowed me with characteristics I thought I lacked—speed, and the ability to slip away, shimmering, if someone tried to squash me. I wanted to be like them, but I was afraid they would make fun of me for it. I never saw another white person scrawling "A.K.A." (also known as) on her books. So I kept my nickname a secret, something I wrote only in the diary that I had started keeping at home.

I noticed that the black kids dressed differently than I did. My fashion world was ruled by the hippie look—fringed leather jackets, torn bellbottoms, muslin shirts, and love beads. Our fashion heroes were the characters in *The Partridge Family* and *The Brady Bunch*, who were far from being hippies but still managed to look groovy. Once the weather cooled off, I usually wore desert boots, Levi jeans or corduroys, and a T-shirt or striped rugby shirt to school. My favorite T-shirts advertised Cold Bear or Boone's Farm wine. Looking back, I'm shocked that none of the adults, my mother included, questioned my willingness to walk around advertising a product that was illegal for me to use. My favorite jeans were tie-dyed purple and yellow, with yellow buttons to close the fly. Second best were orange velour bellbottoms with yellow pockets and yellow buttons.

Instead of wearing scruffy jeans and T-shirts, the black kids actually dressed up for school. Black boys liked to wear pants with three or four buttons on the side of the waistband, imitation-satin dress shirts in a coordinating color, and "elevator" shoes. Black girls wore similar shirts, often with denim skirts and black Converse high-top sneakers.

The most popular black hairdo was the Afro, the fuller the better. For an accent, some girls and boys added a dab of red hair dye. On rainy days, the black kids warned each other, "Your hair gon' fall!" and frantically covered their heads with their textbooks or even old plastic bags. I had no idea why this was so distressing, because the only white people I knew who cared about their hairdos getting wet were old ladies with beehive styles. Cornrows were also popular, mostly with girls. If someone came to school with a particularly elaborate set of braids, she would be asked with admiration, "Who plait your hair?" Usually, an older sister or an aunt had done it.

The white boys with permissive parents grew their hair down to their shoulders. The fashionable white girls ironed their hair so it fell straight and smooth from a part in the center, just like Marcia Brady on *The Brady Bunch*. The black girls were fascinated by any white girl's hair, especially if it was blonde. The first time a girl came up behind me in the hall and started stroking my head, I flinched. But I was afraid she would pull my hair or hit me if I told her to stop. Almost every day, a black girl touched my hair. I learned to put up with it, but I didn't like it.

Once at recess, I worked up the nerve to ask Denise, a black girl in several of my classes, if I could feel her Afro. I rubbed my hands across the top two or three times. I thought it would feel like steel wool, but it was much softer.

The boys and girls in the cool crowd playfully shoved each other and acted upset if the shoves were a little too hard. If they went together, they walked together in the halls and sometimes sneaked kisses under the outdoor stairwell leading from the playground to the industrial arts room. I had no clue what they did after school. My sister's classmates from TJ went to the Lafayette Pharmacy for ice cream and Cokes. I never once saw a black kid in there.

I was attracted to the black crowd's energy. I hated my whiteness for preventing my access to them. I hated the sound of my voice, so proper and schoolmarmish, and my stiff body and silky hair. I wanted to carry myself with pride through the halls, belting out the Motown hits and not caring if I was off-key. I wanted to plait my hair in cornrows with beads at the end of each one and proudly swing my head as I laughed with my friends. But I knew I never could. That would be crossing over, turning my back on my identity, becoming "vanilla fudge." A lot of kids put "Black Is Beautiful" stickers on their notebooks and purses. I saw it everywhere. I believed it. But it wasn't my color.

Self-Segregation

No matter what the court said, separation was the operative principle at our school. When widespread busing began in 1971, the year I started sixth grade at Binford, Richmond middle schools cancelled after-school activities, including sports, clubs, and dances. The reason, we were told, was to avoid fights. I think the real reason was to avoid too much contact between the races. This was classic political maneuvering by the white superintendent of schools: the law said that desegregation had to take place during school hours but said nothing about the rest of the day. The result was a school that never felt like a community, because we never had a chance to do anything but go to classes together.

By responding to the court orders with resentment and foot-dragging, the school administrators bollixed the responsibility they were given. I suspect that their behavior reflected old fears about race mixing ruining the established southern social order. Not once did our school sponsor a special program or an assembly designed to help us get to know one another and learn to work together. The inclusive slogans and programs now commonplace in my children's schools—respecting human differences, celebrating diversity, teaching tolerance—were simply inconceivable back then. Administrators went through the motions, did the minimum, and left children to work out the details.

The cafeteria was divided in half, the boys on one side, the girls on the other, the hot lunch line in the middle. I sat with the other white girls eating lunch at our assigned time, our table the only cluster of white people in the room. I remember only one white girl who sat with black girls. She used the same slang and wore the black fashions, right down to her Converse high top sneakers. Everyone called her vanilla fudge, even to her face.

Sharon, a black girl, started sitting with us because she knew us from our classes. Compared to a lot of the black girls, she looked old-fashioned—her hair bunched into two ponytails instead of combed into an Afro, her dresses below the knee, her blouses baggy.

One day, she sat down, opened her lunch, and kept her head down. When she looked up again, tears were sliding down her face.

"What's wrong?" Loretta asked. Loretta was the other white girl in my gym class, which gave us a bond, though I disliked her bossiness. She had thin, blonde hair that framed a pink face, and she was the self-appointed expert on makeup and boys.

"The other black girls asked why I sit here," Sharon finally admitted. "They said, 'Do you think you're too good for us?'"

Rosalyn, one of the other white girls at the table, said, "You're our friend, right? They don't own you."

Sharon sat with us a few more days, then gave up and started sitting with other black girls again. I imagine they teased her relentlessly, accusing her of being an Oreo (black outside, white inside, the opposite of vanilla fudge) and a snob. No one attempted to change tables after that.

It was an unwritten rule among the black students that getting too friendly with white people was inappropriate. In the 1960s, the black power movement had splintered off the civil rights movement, eventually taking over the leadership of the Student Non-Violent Coordinating Committee. It grew into a national crusade for black self-determination. Even though its influence was waning somewhat by the early 1970s, a lot of my classmates wore the black power fist on T-shirts, as well as on the plastic handles of their Afro combs. Black power instructed black people to find leadership within their own community and to reject the involvement and help of white people, no matter how sympathetic.

As a child, I could not understand the positive message of black power; I just saw the symbols and felt the rejection. My liberal friends around Boston are surprised to hear that I never made one black friend at school. I joked around with some of the girls in my classes, but I never once was invited to anyone's house. Then again, I never invited a black girl to my house after school. One reason was practical. I never saw a black person ride my school bus; I'm not sure anyone was allowed to switch from one bus to another. Even if a black girl did get to my house, how would she have gotten home afterwards? Her parents would have had to be willing to drive across the invisible lines dividing the neighborhoods, putting themselves at risk for being pulled over by a zealous policeman who spotted a black driver in the wrong part of town.

Even if these practical problems could have been solved, we were all following the unwritten social etiquette about getting too friendly. In a school where a few black children were bused in for integration, a white child might feel virtuous and open-minded be-friending a black child. A black child at my school had no incentive to befriend me. I was not a charity case. Nor, as a white person, was I downtrodden. A black girl who was nice to me might feel like she was sucking up to whitey. My presence at her home after school might make her family and neighbors uncomfortable. My mother, liberal as she was, probably wouldn't have wanted to drive alone to pick me up in a black neighborhood, especially after dark. As a white person, I was treated warily, no matter how friendly or open-minded I might be.

Separate Soundtracks

The soundtrack for the black kids at Binford came from Curtis Mayfield, Smokey Robinson, the Temptations, Sly and the Family Stone, Diana Ross and the Supremes, and Aretha Franklin. The students celebrated the soul music that was finally crossing over onto the local Top 40 radio stations and being added to jukeboxes all over the city. The movie *Shaft* rocketed Isaac Hayes, who wrote the theme song, to superstardom in our school. Curtis Mayfield, who wrote "Superfly," was equally popular.

In this context, the Binford orchestra that I played in was a pitiful anachronism. Only seven students, all of us white, played in the orchestra. The teacher, Mr. Watson, was also white, probably in his late twenties, and played bass in the Richmond Symphony. He tried to be cool by wearing thick sideburns, purple shirts, and psychedelic ties, which he never bothered to knot. We rehearsed in a converted storage closet with an entrance out the school's back door, down a set of stairs from the playground.

I had started learning how to play the violin in fifth grade. My mother refused to let me take the drum lessons I asked for, insisting instead that I learn to use the violin that she had played in school. Maybe because the violin was a second choice, I never liked it that much. I slouched when I played. My notes screeched.

Mr. Watson tried to make things interesting by giving us some lively music by Mozart and Bach. He even passed out sheet music of two Beatles hits, "Yesterday" and "Eleanor Rigby." But the class dragged when he was working with individual players. Some of the boys and I disrupted everyone by plucking *The Twilight Zone* theme song on our instruments or rosining our bows so vigorously that the loose horsehairs danced.

I shared a music stand with Sandra, the girl I had known at Mary Munford. Though she was shy at first, our camaraderie as the only white girls in some of our classes had helped me appreciate her sensitivity and subtle humor. She drew a chart of the seating arrangement in one of our classrooms: row after row of filled-in circles with an arrow pointing to "them," then two empty circles with an arrow pointing to "us." She was also the one who wandered down the hall with me one slow day to explore a hidden storage area. Inside, we uncovered a dusty painting of Binford that was so old that the boys in it all wore knickers with suspenders.

"Look," Sandra said, peering over my shoulder. "It has to be old. Everyone's white!" After we stopped laughing, we decided to tell Mr. Watson about our discovery. He told us to turn in the picture at the office.

Principal Harper not only cleaned up the drawing, he also had it framed and hung in the hall outside. I was kind of proud that Sandra and I had found it, but I also felt a bit wistful whenever I saw it. Those children had no idea what kind of upheaval was coming to their school.

Right before Christmas, Mr. Watson sent a group of us into the halls to play Christmas carols outside of the classrooms. The first time we tried to play "Silent Night," another violin player, the class clown, nodded his head to keep time so vigorously that I started laughing and couldn't finish the song. Then we settled down to play "O Christmas Tree" and "We Three Kings." The teachers let their classes come into the hall and listen. There was a ring of black faces around us, seven white students playing holiday songs on our instruments. Everyone listened quietly as the notes echoed down the corridor. It was a bizarre moment of grace.

Everyone had a different reaction to the concert we played for the Christmas assembly. The orchestra marched onstage to play a Bach fugue and other classical pieces. We had worked hard on the program and probably sounded about as good as we ever would. Most of the black kids fidgeted and stared into space. We walked offstage to a polite spatter of applause.

Then the band, also led by Mr. Watson, came on. Most of the players were black, probably because saxophone and trumpet music seemed like lots more fun than the classical music of stringed instruments. They could play jazz, which grew out of black after-hours clubs, creating heroes like Dizzy Gillespie and Charles Mingus. Classical music came from the royal palaces of Vienna and other European capitals, the stuffy province of men in powdered wigs and ladies in corsets. The Herbie Hancock tune the school band played was riveting. By the end, everyone was dancing in the aisles and shouting for an encore.

I watched from behind the stage, amazed. I realized at that moment that I wanted to be playing one of the funky instruments, not the tiresome violin. I wanted to be part of the group that made people dance and cheer, not the one that made people yawn. After the concert, I wiped the rosin off my violin with a rag, stuffed it into the instrument case, and closed the snaps.

To give up the violin and start playing a jazz instrument seemed too much like trying to dance to Sly and the Family Stone in my basement. I ended up teaching myself how to play my mother's old guitar, deciphering the chord charts that led me to sing along with mournful southern folk tunes like "East Virginia" or "Angel from Montgomery." I settled for Joan Baez and Bonnie Raitt as musical role models because Herbie Hancock and Ella Fitzgerald felt off-limits to me.

In the Classrooms

In a way, the schoolwork was the easy part. It was abstract, something that required concentration, something that distracted me from feeling so white. My mother expected me to take school seriously and make good grades, just as she had done. She was always proud when my sister made the honor roll at TJ; I was supposed to do the same at Binford, and I usually did.

My teachers, some black, some white, did not seem to play racial favorites in class. They focused on teaching. Mr. Palmer, who taught American history, was young, black, and cool. He could get away with wearing pink Oxford shirts, loafers, and wide, striped ties. He made us all write a composition from the points of view of a plantation owner and a slave about to be freed in 1865. He also asked us to pick a side from the Civil War (which he did not call The War Between the States) and justify our choice. Showing my liberal upbringing, I sided with the Union, though I did point out that I would have a dilemma if the rest of my family wanted to side with the South.

Another day, Mr. Palmer showed a Bill Cosby film about the "lost, stolen, or strayed" aspects of black history. We learned about leaders like Booker T. Washington and Frederick Douglass. Toward the end of the film, an elementary-school-aged black boy stood up and announced, "I am Afro-American and I'm proud!"

This was the first time a teacher had shown me the black perspective on history. My parents had made sure I knew all about Martin Luther King—in fact, our elementary school in Chicago was cancelled the day of his funeral to keep the city quiet. But Mr. Palmer was the first one to make me realize that Virginia plantation life was not just a well-organized enterprise for growing tobacco. However, he had to be careful not to seem too militant in Mr. Harper's school. He said nothing about the Black Panthers or Malcolm X.

Most of my white teachers at Binford were nearing retirement and perhaps were reassigned to a majority-black school so they wouldn't have to endure what was perceived as a hardship for too many years. The young, white teachers probably got preference to stay in the majority-white schools, where they might have longer careers.

Mrs. Gregg, my homeroom and social studies teacher, combed her gray hair into waves across the top of her head and wore her horn-rim glasses on a chain around her neck. She wrote in every girl's autograph book, "May you always be the same with the exception of your name." One day, as I lingered after class, gathering up my books, she said wistfully, "I used to really enjoy teaching."

Startled, I looked up. Her hands were on her large hips, and she was staring out the window. She had spent her entire career teaching white students. Now, she had to accommodate black kids, who probably made her nervous.

"I didn't have to worry so much about discipline. The students were so polite, so well-behaved. Here," she paused, gesturing around at the empty desks, "well, here, anything goes."

I didn't know how to answer her, so I shrugged.

Students at Binford were divided into four teams according to academic ability, which was the school's way of tracking us. The teachers never gave us labels, but we all knew there was a dumb team, a smart team, and two in between. I was on the so-called smart team. There were more white kids on my team than on the others, perhaps because we scored well on standardized tests, perhaps because the white principal wanted a group of us to show off as the best students.

In class, students seemed more sensitive to race than the teachers. One of the smartest kids on my team was a light-skinned black boy with wire-rimmed glasses. He usually wore a white, button-down shirt and dark slacks, just like a businessman. In math class, while I erased my papers so many times I made holes in them, he always knew the right answers. Classmates of both races always marveled at his ability, as if it was such a surprise to find a brilliant black boy.

Liz was on the so-called dumb team. She didn't make good grades, but I never thought of her as dumb. She just didn't like to read or do her homework as much as I did. With a pencil, she could sketch and cartoon her way through any class that bored her.

Even though I was on the smart team, my math class gave me

trouble. The white teacher, newly married, just out of college, and with braces that made her lisp, probably got stuck with Binford as her first job. She tried to introduce us to algebra, but I just couldn't follow her. To my great amazement, Suzanne rescued me.

She stepped in one night when I came into the kitchen to ask Mom for help.

"Let's see what you have," said Suzanne. Then she got out a pencil and a sheet of scrap paper.

"Here's what you do. Let's say x has the value of 10," and she walked me right through the equation so I finally understood it. Mom stopped putting away the clean dishes to smile at us.

Suzanne made it her special project to help me after that. Pulling a chair up to the oak desk in my room, she would lean over, her shoulder-length hair brushing my notebook paper, patiently explaining x, y, and other mysteries. She probably liked feeling superior to me because math came so naturally to her. Still, I was grateful.

Once in a while, I would sit on the Indian rug under the window in Suzanne's room, just before she turned out the lights to go to bed. It felt like a secret lair with her posters of Woodstock and the Beatles, their faces inside a peace sign, decorating the walls. We talked a little about school. Most of her white classmates were planning to finish high school at TJ, even though the buses each day brought loads of black kids. The black kids, she said, took over certain tables in the cafeteria and cut class to smoke reefer in the bleachers. They were planning their own prom, boycotting the one the white students would attend. Suzanne was busy applying to colleges. Her first choice was "as far from Richmond as Mother will let me go," she said.

My Flag, My Shame

Maybe if one of my teachers had explained the African American view of the Confederacy instead of shunning topics with any hint of racial controversy, I would have been prepared to resist the sales pitch of the man in an Allman Brothers Band T-shirt. I was at the Virginia State Fair, and it was the fall of 1972, my seventh grade year at Binford. It was my last stop on a long night of prowling around the midway with the Zellers. We had gorged ourselves with popcorn and cotton candy, ridden the dizzying Round-Up, and thrown darts at balloons, hoping for a prize. The man, perched on a box behind a folding table, his hair clasped back in a ponytail, watched me eyeing the array of patches he sold. There was a peace sign, an assortment of psychedelic mushrooms, and a giant marijuana leaf. He picked up a checkered flag crisscrossed with the Confederate flag and waved it above the table.

"Go Confederates!" he said, his teeth bright as the lights on the ride whirling outside the tent. "Get it?"

I was at the age when a man's smile could make a difference.

"Yeah!" I said, and smiled back. "How much?"

"For you?" he said, eyeing my sister's hand-me-down denim jacket, my wad of frizzy hair, my dime store earrings, my dogged determination to fit in somewhere, anywhere. "Tell you what. Two dollars."

I reached into the pocket of my Levi's jeans and handed over the money.

"That'll look real nice on your jacket there," he said, packing the patch in a paper bag and smiling again. "Come back and see me sometime."

I took the bag, and my cousins, impatient to leave, didn't ask to see it. In the back seat of the Chevy station wagon, wedged between Naomi and Sammy, I rubbed the patch in the dark. Finally, I felt like a Richmonder.

My mother made no comment as I left the next morning, the new patch on the front of my jacket. Despite her support for integration,

70

she was too much of a southerner to see the flag as anything objectionable. I practically strutted up to the door of the school instead of doing my usual hangdog scuttle.

I hadn't gotten twenty feet inside when a black girl I didn't know shoved me. Her Afro puffed up like a cloud of steam above her head. She narrowed her eyes, jabbing me where the patch was sewn on, cursed at me, and stalked off.

Stunned, I continued into homeroom, where two boys went silent and glared at me as I walked by.

It took Denise, the black girl who had once let me touch her Afro, to tell me what I had done wrong. She was one of the few girls who seemed comfortable enough to be consistently friendly with me. After lunch that day, Denise pulled me into a corner of the cracked and weedy asphalt that passed as our playground.

"That flag on your jacket," she said, the usual teasing edge gone from her voice. "It's got to go."

My stomach somersaulted. Still, I didn't know exactly what I had done wrong. I waited for her to say more.

"You really don't get it, do you?" she said impatiently.

Denise and I had just stumbled into the no-man's-land between what busing was supposed to achieve and one of the nation's most potent symbols of racial misunderstanding. As twelve-year-olds, we were supposed to be more open to social change, but we were also woefully lacking any kind of perspective on history.

"Don't you see we would still be slaves if they won?" she said.

No answer I gave could possibly stanch the shame that flooded my face.

I wadded up the jacket, stuffed it into my knapsack, and didn't wear it on the bus that afternoon, even though I was shivering. When I got home, I took out my mother's manicure scissors and cut out every one of my careful stitches. I shoved the patch into the back of my drawer. I certainly couldn't wear it again. Yet I also couldn't bring myself to throw it out. I had so carefully chosen it—a star-crossed reminder of all I still had to learn about American history.

Girl Talk

In the dark, in the wooden seats of the auditorium at Binford, the film jittered through the projector. All the girls were watching, the boys sent upstairs to their own special assembly with the male gym teacher. On the screen, a girl in a plaid skirt and saddle shoes, her blond hair curled into a flip, walked into her living room. Her mother, a navy blue dress smoothed over her knees, looked up from her knitting.

"Guess what, Mom!" the girl announced, smiling.

"You're menstruating, dear!" said the mother, as if that's the first thing that any mother would guess out loud like that.

"Why, yes!" said the girl. "How did you know?"

"Oh, sometimes mothers know things like that," she said.

In the auditorium, some girls snickered. Mrs. Martin, the guidance counselor, paced the aisles in her white blouse and plaid skirt, her heels ticking officiously. I elbowed Liz and rolled my eyes. Liz and I sat in a row with about two dozen white girls; the rest of the auditorium was filled with black girls. The only other white person that I remember in the room was Mrs. Martin.

The mother showed her daughter a sanitary napkin, then told her to wash carefully on the days of her period. Their bathroom had a plush toilet seat cover and matching wallpaper with flowers on it. The girl looked shocked when her classmate called her period "the curse."

"It's not the curse," the narrator said in a voice-over. "It's perfectly normal."

"Yeah, and perfectly embarrassing," I muttered to Liz, who had to cover her mouth to stifle her laughter.

We were all watching the same film, but neither the script nor the teacher helped me to feel I had anything common with the black girls who were also going through the awkward transition to womanhood. The staff at the school handled the film the way they handled so many other things—by following the requirements of the curriculum, but backing off from any real discussion. Who in our auditorium could possibly identify with the characters in the film? Everyone in the film was white, dressed in their 1950s fashions, relics from the era when schools were still segregated and Elvis's dancing was still risqué. The worst thing the girls in the film had to worry about was how to politely decline swimming invitations during the days of their periods.

A counselor or teacher who felt more comfortable in front of an integrated group might have acknowledged the absurdity of the film's old-fashioned script. She might have asked us to give practical advice to each other, especially about confronting the obnoxious boys who rummaged through our purses, holding up any sanitary supplies they found. That could have helped bridge some of the divisions between us. Mrs. Martin just showed the film, left no time for questions, and sent us back to class.

What did the film's producers know of the racial tensions that kept girls from talking to each other about the most basic of female functions? About squirming through cramps because I thought it was worse to tell a black girl than to tough it out? About tying a sweater around my waist because I hated the bathroom so much, I sometimes ended up with stained pants? The stalls of the girls' bathroom had no trash receptacles. This was probably a simple oversight, but it made discretion impossible because we had to walk out to a trash can that was in the corner of the bathroom where the most hostile girls had staked out their turf. At a different school, the girls might have complained to each other, and then urged the bravest one to go ask the school nurse for better trash disposal. Instead, no one said anything and nothing changed.

At home, my mother stashed her feminine supplies way back in her closet, never leaving a trace of her period in the bathroom. She delivered the little information she shared in a detached, clinical tone that instantly squelched my questions. My older sister, obsessed with privacy, said nothing. My white girlfriends were the only people I knew who would talk about periods at all, and we usually joked to cover our discomfort. In my situation, no matter what the film's narrator said, I indeed felt cursed to be a young woman.

Ebony and Ivory

Like most twelve-year-old girls, I schemed incessantly about how to find a boyfriend. Desegregation brought a whole new level of complication to the possibilities. Virginia's miscegenation laws had been taken off the books in 1967, just four years before I started being bused. The test case that reached the Supreme Court, *Loving v. Virginia*, was brought by an interracial couple who wanted their marriage recognized instead of outlawed in Virginia.

The Rolling Stones celebrated interracial sex in "Brown Sugar," but "Brother Louie," the popular and ominous song about a "black as night" girl and her "whiter than white" boyfriend who was violently disowned by his parents, was more reflective of southern attitudes. School authorities made sure we had as little social contact as possible by canceling school dances and sports—a response that was similar to Richmond's removal of benches at public parks after the Civil Rights Act of 1964.

There were unwritten rules about interracial interaction between girls and boys, enforced by both races. The black girls who came to school wearing Michael Jackson buttons and Jackson 5 T-shirts brushed me off when I said I was a fan, too. Back then, Michael Jackson still had dark skin, a flat nose, and kinky hair. The girls also ignored me when I tried to jump into their playground discussions about which Jackson brother was the cutest. They asked me instead about the comparable white-boy group, the Osmond Brothers. I thought the lead singer, Donnie, was a ridiculous teeny-bopper. Nonetheless, when Loretta found his mailing address in the back of a fan magazine, I joined the girls at the white table in the lunchroom in writing fan letters to him. "Dear Donnie, I know you've never heard of me, but I really like your music," I lied. None of us received a response.

At our white table in the cafeteria, the other girls and I used to ask each other to guess which boys we liked. We always rotated through the same five or six white boys in our classes. My favorite was the smart-aleck Adam, who teased me about everything from the color of my socks to my chest size, but he kept things interesting. When Liz and a gum-snapping brunette on her team named Darlene liked the same boy, Darlene challenged Liz to a dress-up contest. Here's what I remember: the boy was supposed to choose the girl who looked better that day. Liz complained that it was stupid, but she did wear a dress on the appointed day instead of her usual jeans and peasant blouses. He picked the other girl, which annoyed Liz. She ended up saying that he wasn't worth it, anyway.

Loretta was the only one of us who actually found a boyfriend within the school. Terry, his chin-length bangs sweeping across his freckled forehead, was willing to walk with her in the hall between classes. His high-water bell-bottoms revealed his white socks with every step. He even made her a bracelet in the school's shop class and had it engraved with his name on one side, hers on the other.

One day, I decided to reveal that I liked Dion, a dark-skinned boy in my homeroom who was built like a basketball player. He liked to sing while he beat time on the desk until Miss Gregg shushed him. After he had to stop, I would move my hands silently above my desk to let him know I wished he could keep going. We'd grin at each other.

I made every girl keep guessing until she gave up. Then I announced, "Dion!"

Everyone fell silent for what seemed like several minutes.

Finally, Loretta said, "You didn't tell us he was black!"

"So?" I said.

"You're asking for trouble," Loretta said, straightening her shoulders with self-importance.

I hated to admit it, but she was right. The trouble could come in many forms. First of all, there was my mother. She had once told me that when she was a student at the University of Michigan, a black man from the Caribbean had asked her for a date. She ended up turning him down. She remembered telling him, "I'm from the South. There would be too many problems if I got serious with you and tried to bring you home."

I had no intention of getting serious in the sixth grade, but I truly didn't know what Mom would say if I told her I wanted to "go with" a black boy. I pictured her wrinkling her brow and saying, "Well, there could be many, many problems." But I was also fairly sure she would not forbid me. That wasn't her style. Anyway, how could she, since I had grown up playing with black children in Chicago, and since she was the one who wanted me to stay in the public schools?

In Chicago, when Dad headed the family, black children from the neighborhood had trooped in and out of our yard, our kiddie pool, our living room. I doubted that Dad, the legal aid lawyer who was proud to represent clients of color, would have prevented me from going out with someone black, either.

Even if my family was likely to be tolerant, however, I worried that the black girls would insult me and threaten to beat me up for taking one of their boys. They didn't even want me to write a fan letter to Michael Jackson!

I'm not sure Dion would have been happy to hear that I liked him, either. Black boys had to be extremely careful around white girls. It was the southern belief since the time of slavery that white women had to be protected from the uncontrollable lust of black men. The consequences of even a small, flirtatious act could be deadly. In one of the best-known examples, black teenager Emmett Till was lynched for whistling at a white Mississippi shopkeeper in 1955.

If a black man wanted to show any kind of attraction to a white woman, it had to be clandestine. At school, that meant the black boys didn't touch my hair—something the girls did almost every day—as I walked through the halls. None of them teased me about my growing chest size or my frizzy hair the way the white boys did. In fact, none of them spoke much to me at all. They knew the unwritten rules.

Principal Harper made his fears clear on the sweltering day in May that I decided to wear shorts to school. There was no official dress code, though I had never seen anyone wearing shorts. I can't remember why I wanted to challenge things; I probably felt it was unfair that we could wear pants but not shorts. I chose what I thought were my most conservative shorts, the loose ones with a geometric print, not the tight, purple hot pants with orange pockets or the cutoffs with frayed bottoms. Mom always went to work before I left for school, so she wasn't home to object.

I was called out of my first-period class and sent to Mrs. Martin.

She frowned from her swivel chair and tapped a ruler against her desk. I shivered in her air-conditioned office.

"Come here," she said, then held a ruler against my thigh to measure the distance between my knee and the bottom of my shorts. As she leaned over, I could smell her perspiration cutting through her perfumed deodorant and see the strands of gray in her brown hair, which curled toward her face.

"I don't know," she said, a rueful smile playing around her pink-glossed lips. "Mrs. Snead?" she called her colleague.

I had to make the same humiliating twirl in front of the other guidance counselor, also white. The other counselor shook her head in Mrs. Martin's direction. "I don't think so."

"Too far above the knee," declared Mrs. Martin. "Go on home and change, and then you can come back to school."

I could feel myself starting to cry. I didn't think I had done anything wrong. Besides, Mom hated being called at work. She gave my sister and me strict orders never to disturb her unless it was an emergency.

"I, I, I can't," I stammered. "My mother is at work. She can't leave and pick me up."

"What about your father?"

"My father is . . . he . . . well," I said, feeling even worse, "he died when I was seven."

Mrs. Martin narrowed her eyes at me, too indignant to show any sympathy. "We're going to call your mother. We can't allow you to stay here looking like that."

I sat in a slippery leather chair while she dialed Grace House and waited for Mom to leave her classroom and come to the phone.

Their conversation went back and forth, ending with Mrs. Martin's tight face and clipped voice: "All right, Mrs. Silverstein, I'll set up the appointment."

She hung up the phone and glared at me.

"All right, you have permission to stay for the rest of the day. But for your own good, don't you ever wear shorts to this school again. And don't plan on riding the bus this afternoon. Your mother will be taking you home. She's coming in to see Mr. Harper."

I nodded, afraid my voice would quaver if I talked.

"Here's your pass," she said. "Go back to class now."

I worried all day that I was in big, big trouble.

When the last bell rang, I gathered up my books and went down to the office. I waited on a bench outside. When Mom came out, she shook hands with Mr. Harper.

"Thank you for meeting with me," she said. "Come on, Clara, I'll take you home."

Mom walked so briskly I could barely keep up with her. As soon as we left the building, I couldn't contain myself. "What did he say? Am I getting suspended?"

"They have no right to tell you what to wear in a public school," Mom snapped. "I told Mr. Harper he was treading on thin ice, getting too close to your First Amendment rights."

"Which First Amendment right?" I said.

"The right to free expression," she said.

"Oh," I answered, unsure of what to say next.

Who was right, who was wrong in this case? My challenge to the rules, whether they were unfair or not, made me feel more ashamed than heroic.

My mother unlocked her rust-colored Chevrolet Nova and we immediately rolled down the windows to let the hot air out.

As we drove home, Mom chose her words carefully. "You know, it is wrong for a public school to set a dress code. But Mr. Harper runs a tight ship. He is afraid that the boys will bother you. I think, in this situation, you're better off not wearing shorts to school again. Save them for knock-around on the weekends."

I could tell from the tightness of her hands against the steering wheel that she was still angry—not at me, but at Mr. Harper. She only stood five feet three and weighed 120 pounds, but her "I-mean-business" voice could pack a punch.

Years later, she told me the rest of the conversation: Mr. Harper said that boys might find girls in tank tops and shorts too "stimulating." Then he pointed to a corner in the hall between his office and the nurse's room. "Boys could take girls into dark corners like that and rape them," he said.

He didn't say "black boys" and "white girls," but it didn't take much for my mother to fill in the blanks.

Now I admire her for standing up to him—as a single parent, no less—and for defending her opinion and not falling prey to his stereotypes. At the time, I was overwhelmed by conflicting forces: my desire to challenge what I thought was a petty rule, my shame that the counselor measured my bare thighs with her ruler, my horror that the response dragged in the principal as well as my mother. Because the dress code seemed to be a smokescreen for white fears of interracial contact, I had stumbled into something far beyond what I had intended. I never tried to wear shorts to Binford again, though I did wear skirts that revealed just as much of my thighs.

The White Boys

Billy, one of my white classmates, and I sat on the floor of the hall at Binford, banished from seventh-grade library time because we had switched the radio from Muzak to WRVQ, the new FM rock station. Alone, away from the banter—his teasing that my baggy, corduroy pants made me look like a boy, my retort that he wouldn't know what a girl looked like if she stood in front of him naked—I didn't know what to say. He was white, Jewish, one of the boys I was supposed to like. But I knew he always went out with girls from private schools. I didn't rate.

He cocked his head against the tile wall, his hair coiling above his scalp, and leered at me. He was close enough for me to see the hint of a moustache on his upper lip.

"So, Clara, are you afraid to do things with guys?"

Instinctively, I pulled my knees up to hide my chest while I tried to come up with an answer that would sound like I fell into the safe middle ground between a prude and a slut.

"Of course not," I bluffed, squaring my shoulders with what I thought was toughness. "Why should I be?"

"You shouldn't," he said. He looked like he was going to say more, but the librarian called us back in.

A few weeks later, I decided I liked Clyde, whose spiky brown hair, blue eyes, and sassiness first started attracting my attention at recess. Short and wiry, he seemed to be able to magically insert himself into a knot of boys and come out with control of the ball during kickball games. When I wanted to see if he liked me, I chose Loretta to ask him. She was the most attuned to gossip and the least afraid to ask a boy his opinion of a girl.

After lunch the next day, Loretta cornered me on the ramp leading out to the playground.

"I talked to Clyde," she said.

"Oh?" I asked, trying to sound nonchalant, though my heart started banging in my ears.

She tossed her bangs out of her eyes. She had brushed her eyelids with sparkly blue shadow up to her brows.

"Oh, Clara, you're not going to like this," she said, giggling nervously.

My stomach clenched. "What, he doesn't like me?" I said, prepared to shrug it off.

Loretta nodded her head and said, "He told me, 'I wouldn't get within ten feet of that dirty Jew.'"

The bottom fell out of my stomach. All I could do was gape at her while she kept giggling.

Wordlessly, I turned and walked outside. I leaned over the metal drinking fountain near the alley, blinking until the tears cleared and I could lift up my head again. I was furious with Loretta, and I didn't want to believe that Clyde had said what Loretta had reported. I still liked him, in spite of everything.

I wondered if I could do something to change his mind. I wondered if Loretta had made up the story just to keep me away from him because she wanted him for herself. I was the only Jewish girl in the school, and calling me a dirty Jew eliminated me as a competitor. But it must have been true; in my autograph book at the end of the seventh grade Clyde wrote, "To a weird Jew. Have fun this summer."

Would one of the Jewish boys have defended me had he known what Clyde said? Most of them were too busy teasing me. They and the rest of the white boys at school ignored the southern social code that ladies should be protected. Their comments in my autograph book from that year reveal just how little support I could count on from these fellow white students:

"To a girl who is starting to grow."

"To a girl with big ideas and small other things."

A black boy, observing my orthodontia, at least managed to say something positive: "Good luck with the brace on your face. Because I know there is at least one smile in the white race!"

Filmstrip in the Dark

Walter sat in front of me in seventh-grade American history, his shoulders shaking with suppressed laughter as he drew cartoons in the margins of my textbook. He often slipped me cough drops and sticks of Juicy Fruit gum, contraband in the classrooms. He kept his Afro short and tidy instead of letting it flatten on the sides or catch stray pieces of lint. He smelled like lemon oil.

One day when Mr. Palmer turned off the lights to show a filmstrip, Walter's hand inched across the top of my desk, grazed my pinky, then came to rest on top of mine. Its heat seared me. The top of his hand was the color of hot cocoa, though it looked gray in the light of the images projected onto the pull-down screen.

Heart pounding, I looked around to see if anyone noticed us. Sandra, who sat next to me, was drawing flowers on her book cover. Billy had his head down on his desk, his eyes closed. Some of the other kids were yawning.

At this point, I must have made a decision to let him keep his hand there, but I don't remember what I was thinking in the dizzying seconds after he touched my hand. At our table in the cafeteria, I had been willing to test the boundaries when I admitted to liking a black boy in my homeroom. Now I was willing step farther with Walter, a boy I did find attractive. I liked the frisson of doing something illicit, wanted to see what would happen.

What motivated Walter? That he liked me was almost beside the point. It was too dangerous for him to come out and tell me. He had to find a safe way to test the limits. It was brave, and also brilliant, of him to slide his hand across the desk. He counted on me not to make a scene in the hushed classroom. If I refused to take his hand, all he had to do was turn around and pretend nothing happened.

I carefully slid my textbooks into a barricade next to our hands, so nobody would see. Walter slipped his thumb under my palm, fingers stroking the back of my hand. My fingers nudged his. His head faced the front, eyes on the red and white cloth that Betsy Ross was sewing. I didn't want to look at his face anyway, our hands the only evidence of our sweat commingling, breaking all the taboos.

On and on the chirpy narrator went about Betsy's skills as a seamstress, a beep signaling Mr. Palmer to advance to the next picture. The more the narrator talked, the more ridiculous the filmstrip seemed. What did Betsy know about black boys? Had she ever touched one?

Mr. Palmer, change jingling in his pockets as he paced the room on his long legs, didn't seem to notice. He paused, rubbed the beard on his dark face, then continued. When he walked past us to turn the lights back on, Walter pulled his hand back into his lap. I picked up my pencil and looked down at my notebook. I wondered if I was blushing. I didn't hear whether Mr. Palmer assigned us any homework and had to ask Sandra.

I wondered where else Walter and I could hold hands. The secret burned inside me like a flame that could be blown out by any harsh words, any hostile looks. I liked him, but none of the ordinary rules applied. If he had been white, the next step might have been to walk together in the hall, look for each other on the playground at recess, and sit together to watch the kickball games. If things escalated, he might have called me at home or arranged to meet me after school. However, I had no idea where he lived, what his house looked like, where he hung out after school.

Did I like him enough to hear Sandra warn me, "Watch out!"? To hear Billy and his friends saying, "Ebony and ivory!" everywhere I went? To be stared at and followed when I tried to sit next to him on a bench at the school playground? To have nowhere to go outside of school? I hadn't seen a single mixed-race couple at school, or almost anywhere in Richmond. The only one I could think of was Mom's boss, who was white, and his wife, who was black. But they were old and married. I was twelve and hadn't even kissed anyone yet.

I didn't tell anyone about Walter, not even Liz. I just couldn't face the potential ridicule. I also wanted to keep the whole thing protected from the forces that swirled around us. We could find sweetness, however fleeting, amid the maelstrom. To expose ourselves would surely end everything.

In the classroom it started, and in the classroom it stayed. I held hands with Walter until Mr. Palmer changed the seating chart after Christmas vacation. At first, we smiled at each other from across the room, but after a while I got used to seeing the back of his shirt.

The Fox-Trot, the Cha-Cha

My mother was acting more like a southern lady than a liberal teacher when she signed me up in 1972 for ballroom dance lessons at Miss Virginia Davis's Cotillion. Dance lessons had been part of my mother's upbringing. In an old-fashioned way, she thought I could benefit from the exposure to elite Richmond society. Never mind how useless these lessons were to anyone who attended a desegregated school, where dances were not allowed.

At first I went along with it—the pantyhose, the dresses, the white gloves. I was curious, I suppose, and interested in trying something social outside of school. I was in a carpool with Liz and Annemarie. Even though I still liked Annemarie's spunkiness and sense of humor, we seldom saw each other anymore. She had made a new group of friends at Collegiate, her private school.

On the first night of cotillion, the three of us walked into a ballroom with a scuffed wooden floor. When the music started, we lined up for the "Grand March," boys on one side of the room, girls on the other. The march matched each of us with a partner.

Miss Davis, her graying curls piled atop her head, stood at the center of the room in a spangled evening gown and pearls. Beaming, she demonstrated the waltz with a dapper, gray-haired partner. Her white pumps clicked out the rhythm as she said: "One two three, one two three, one two three, turn the girl."

At other cotillions, I learned the fox trot, the cha-cha, and the tango. At Christmas there was a Holly Ball, which called for floor-length dresses and nosegays. Most of the other kids—about two hundred in all—went to private schools. There was not a single black kid in the crowd. Some of the girls whispered to each other as they lined up for the Grand March. They counted the boys on the other side, rearranging themselves to try to get a particular partner. I didn't know any of the boys. I was randomly paired with boys who danced with me once or twice, then went off to find one of the blonde girls wearing a plaid kilt and gold knot earrings.

One night, Liz pointed out Judge Merhige's son, who attended

Collegiate with Annemarie. In his suit, tie, and loafers, he looked just like any other preppie. His father had ordered me to go to a school where I was tripped in the halls and spit on in the cafeteria, but had spared his own son that kind of treatment. I glared at him from across the room. I hated Judge Merhige for not making his son go the public schools.

Standing with Liz, I looked around and whispered, "I think we're the only people in here who go to a public school in Richmond."

Liz nodded, then shrugged it off in her usual, easygoing way. I couldn't shrug it off so easily. If any of my dance partners tried to make conversation by asking where I went to school, my answer was a sure turnoff.

"Binford," I would say.

"Where's that?" he would ask.

"In Richmond."

"I've never heard of it."

"It's a public school."

"Oh. Isn't it dangerous?" he might ask, if he asked anything else at all.

I'd clench my jaw and try to pay attention to my feet. Even if I looked like every other girl in my panty hose and party dress, my attendance at a Richmond public school made me a social reject. I was tainted by my association with black kids, something the lace-trimmed white gloves could never cover.

I left cotillion after two years. So did Liz. I saved the white gloves as a souvenir, eventually giving them to my daughter for dress-up. She sometimes puts them on and clacks around her room in high heels announcing, "I'm a lady," a title I never claimed in spite of those lessons.

My parents around the time of their marriage, 1950

Family portrait,
Chicago, 1963

Our integrated kiddie pool in Chicago, July 1964

Ice skating with a neighbor, Chicago, ca. 1967

Family portrait, 1972, four years after my father's death
(*Photograph by Ann F. Oppenhimer*)

Seventh-grade school photo, 1972–73

Richmonders protesting busing
(*Valentine Richmond History Center*)

My bat mitzvah, April 1973

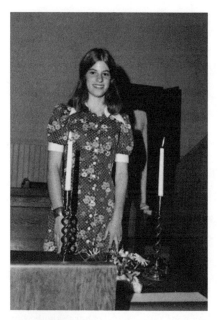

In front of the Virginia State Capitol, February 1976

Awards ceremony for excellent Richmond public high school students, 1978

My graduation from the Open High School, May 1978

Invisible

In the eighth grade, I was reassigned to Hill Middle School, the same school that my mother had attended in the 1930s when it was all white. The Binford building could only accommodate sixth and seventh grades, so all of us had to attend eighth grade elsewhere. Hill was about 85 percent black by the time I arrived in the fall of 1973. It was close enough for me to walk; the black students, and whites who lived farther from school than me, were bused. The building's yellowish brick walls looked grimy up close. Two pine trees as tall as the building's three stories flanked the entrance. Behind the school was an asphalt playground, and across the street was a playing field where Mom had once learned field hockey. The school's asphalt tennis courts were in the next block, across traffic-choked Thompson Street.

Most mornings, I went to school with Liz. Once again, she was not in any of my classes because she was not on the honors track. I was lonelier than ever because there were only two other white girls to sit with in the cafeteria. Most of the white people I knew from Binford had gone to private schools. A lot of the black kids, including Walter, had also been dispersed, mostly reassigned to other Richmond public schools.

When I told my mother that Sandra was transferring into Trinity Episcopal, a new school south of the James River, she shook her head and sighed. Trinity was one of the schools around Richmond that had opened or expanded in response to the busing-fueled demand.

"Private schools give kids lots of book smarts, but no common sense," my mother said. "Those little darlings are so sheltered."

"Don't you think Sandra will have more friends than I do?" I asked. I was pointing out what I saw as an advantage. I didn't care so much about reading Chaucer in English class and being well prepared for the SATs, the educational advantages that private schools were supposed to bestow on me. I wanted a chance to be popular, something that would never happen to me as a white girl at my current school.

"She might, but everyone is the same," my mother said. She also pointed out that most of the private schools in Richmond were Christian. If I became a student, I would have to go to chapel and recite the Lord's Prayer even if I didn't want to.

My mother also objected to paying the tuition, though it was something she could have afforded had she made it a priority. My father's life insurance and my grandmother's resources had left her with enough money to send me to ballet lessons (a waste, as I was so clumsy the teacher cut me from the spring recital) and summer camp.

Her main criticism of private schools had nothing to do with money. Rather, it had to do with my father's ideals.

"The world is not made only for privileged white people, you know," she said.

I certainly had enough evidence that this was true, so I let the subject drop. Sandra was one of the friends I missed most as I yawned my way through French class without anyone to help me make up fake definitions, or as I cowered in the back of the locker room when changing for gym class.

The only bright spot that year was my independent study with a literature specialist from the Richmond public schools. I had started out in Miss Torrey's English class. She squinched her mouth, prefaced every sentence with "aw, uh, aw, uh," and hobbled around the room on legs that looked like they might give out any second. Her idea of a class was telling each of us to read a passage from the textbook aloud and then asking if we had any questions. When I asked if we could ever do any creative writing, she said, "Few students can write any poetry that makes sense, so we won't waste our class time on it."

At dinner, I told Mom what Miss Torrey had said about poetry. My mother knew I liked to write poetry as well as fiction, that I spent hours in my room filling spiral notebooks with my own writing.

She looked up from her salad bowl and said, "This is appalling! How does an English teacher have the right to say such a thing? I'm going to get on the phone and call your principal. He ought to know about something like that."

The next day Mom went to see Mr. Knickerbocker, whom the students nicknamed "Mr. Break-em-back-er" because he didn't mess around when it came to discipline. To my surprise, Mr. Knickerbocker recommended that I work with the citywide literature specialist at her office in the Humanities Center in downtown Richmond, former home of the writer Ellen Glasgow. The City of Richmond had acquired the building a few years earlier and turned it into an arts resource center for the schools. On the premises were a photographer, a filmmaker, a video artist, a musician, a visual artist, and the literary specialist that I would see.

On my first day, I pushed open the front door to a reception desk and a grand stairway ascending to the second floor. On the left was a music room with a bare wood floor, mirrors, and a grand piano in the corner.

The literature specialist, Ruby Norris, had an office adjoining a library filled with books, plants, and double-hung windows. A woman of about fifty with wispy hair dyed blonde, a white blouse, and plaid skirt, Mrs. Norris looked like a schoolmarm. Yet she didn't act stuffy. She smiled as she read the poems I had scrawled.

"Now, tell me what you've been reading," she said.

During our first, brief lesson, she assigned me a novel to read and told me to buy a journal and begin recording anything that struck me as interesting.

After this meeting, once a week I left Hill early and walked down Roseneath Road to Grove Avenue. Here, I caught the Westhampton 16 bus eastbound. The first few times, I felt like I was playing hooky. I had never left school in the middle of the day unless I was sick. Then I began to enjoy the adventure. I soon learned all the landmarks along the route: Beth-El, Richmond's largest synagogue besides the one my family attended; St. Benedict's parochial school, which required boys to wear their hair in buzz cuts and girls to wear plaid skirts and white shirts; and the Virginia Museum. Then came the renovated Fan District homes, with porches ripped off and bricks painted white, green, or pink; the long-haired college students milling around the streets near Virginia Commonwealth University (VCU); Monroe Park, where winos loitered on benches; and finally, my stop at Foushee and Franklin Streets.

In my journal, I wrote about the people I saw on the bus: black domestic workers who huffed up the bus steps, toddlers who cried despite their mothers' annoyed hisses of "shhh!" and laborers who reeked of sweat and cigarettes.

Mrs. Norris photocopied poems by William Carlos Williams to show me simplicity. She sent me to the Humanities Center's writing workshops for teachers, where poets read their own work. I squirmed and felt self-conscious about being the only thirteen-year-old in the room, but I forgot all that when I listened to their words. The images took me into the jungle, the Roman ruins, or whatever they were describing.

Because of the independent study, every day after lunch I went to the library for a study hall. The white librarians, whom I nicknamed Miss Spider and Miss Hard Thing, wore lots of foundation, which caked in their wrinkles and made them look even older than they probably were. Miss Hard Thing's perfume was suffocating. They presided from behind the checkout desk, chatting with each other but glaring at anyone who wasn't sitting quietly at a wooden table. They seemed rattled when anyone asked for help finding a book—and who would, given their reaction? Like Mrs. Gregg at Binford, they seemed upset by having to work with black students. Yet they had to put up with it, because they needed their jobs.

I usually sat alone at a table near the stacks. For the first few minutes, it was quiet, but then a group of black kids regularly came in to socialize. As a white girl, I was invisible to them. When a group sat at my table because the others were full, I pretended to read but couldn't help but listen to them complain about Miss Spider and Miss Hard Thing. I was afraid to laugh with them, because I thought they would get mad at me for eavesdropping.

The black group's horseplay sent Miss Spider and Miss Hard Thing over the edge.

"Where's your paaaaassss?" Miss Hard Thing croaked to each new arrival, her southern drawl stretching out the words.

"Quaaaaah-et!" Miss Spider rasped, only to be interrupted five minutes later by loud guffaws.

"We caaaa-yunnt have that in heeee-ah!" she would try again.

One day, Sondra, a black girl who wore a cigarette behind her ear and a stick of incense in her Afro, bent down and kissed a black boy on the nose.

"Whoooo-eeee!" he exclaimed, and jumped up out of his seat.

Miss Hard Thing was apoplectic. She said, "Whey-ahh ahh you supposed to be right now? We caaa-yunt have this in the library!"

I propped up the journal in front of my face and tried not to let everyone see I was laughing. Sondra, whose hot temper I had observed as she scolded and shoved kids in the cafeteria, might have been insulted and lashed out at me. I was also worried that Miss Hard Thing would start treating me even worse than she already did, and I had to go into the library nearly every day.

I began to feel like I was watching everyone through glass, particularly my black schoolmates. I knew practically nothing of their friendships, their romances, where they lived, or where they went after school to buy candy bars and sodas. I didn't even know most of their names. Yet I overheard all sorts of things, because nobody cared whether I was listening or not. One day, a black girl heard a John Denver tune on a transistor radio, made a face and said to her friend, "That's some tired music."

What an irony that I identified so much with a passage from Ralph Ellison's *Invisible Man* that I copied it into my journal: "I am invisible, understand, simply because people refuse to see me. Like the bodiless heads you see sometimes in circus sideshows, it is as though I have been surrounded by mirrors of hard, distorting glass." He had racism pegged, that was for sure.

Ellison was just one of the black authors I was reading. The English teacher who supervised my independent study showed me poems by Langston Hughes and Lucille Clifton. My mother, always interested in educating herself on racial matters, bought paperbacks of *Manchild in the Promised Land* by Claude Brown, *The Autobiography of Malcolm X*, and *Black Boy* by Richard Wright. My sister and I took turns reading them. I also read *Black like Me* by John H. Griffin and imagined what it would be like to disguise myself as a black girl. I thought it might be a good thing at school, because for once, people would talk to me.

I read and reread the opening chapters of *Malcolm X*, when Malcolm and his friends conk their hair and learn to Lindy-Hop. I also was fascinated by Brown's descriptions of running with a gang in Harlem. Both men made their world sound colorful and fun. Their struggles to find jobs, get respect from Whitey, and escape a life of crime were more sobering. They made it clear that the world was stacked against the black man. Yet I had trouble making the connection between these books and my situation at school. In my world, the black kids were on top and I was on the bottom. I sometimes wondered what it would be like to be blind, to not know any color at all, to live in a world of pure sensation, all social divisions based on a person's looks irrelevant.

"Imagine," I wrote one day, sitting under the pine tree near the entrance of the library, which I had left without permission because I just couldn't stand one more minute of it. "Just ten years ago, this school was lily white. All the girls wore knee-length skirts and bobby socks; all the boys straight leg trousers (jeans unheard of) and crew cuts. Sometimes, I wish one of those students was me! At least I'd know where I was going and exactly what I was about."

I had no place at school, nothing to connect me. I kept writing, my private notebooks the only place I dared say what I noticed, what I felt. Below my numb face, my hips and breasts slowly, almost magically, curved into a woman's shape. This was an embarrassment as well as a source of pride, because boys and men noticed me once I stepped out of school.

In the early 1970s, my mother and my cousins helped start a new, ultraliberal synagogue named Or Ami. Our family membership there gave me a welcome escape from Hill, the school I had started calling, without too much of stretch, "Hell." The services avoided using the word *God* and replaced the traditional liturgy with songs by Bob Dylan and quotes from Dag Hammarskjöld. In 1974, when I was thirteen, I became the first member to celebrate a Bat Mitzvah. It was not just a matter of learning enough Hebrew to recite prayers and read from the Torah. I also had to pick a theme for my service. I chose loneliness, in part to avoid what I thought were cliché topics like creativity or friendship, in part because I thought my personal theme song was Simon and Garfunkel's "I Am a Rock."

"Interesting," said the rabbi. "I think it has real possibilities. Let's talk about it." His eyes drilled into mine. "Do you feel lonely when you think about your father?"

I squirmed at the rabbi's question. Anything I felt about my father was so deeply buried I barely noticed it myself, much less dredged it up to discuss with someone else.

"I don't know," I said, staring at the white shag carpet so he wouldn't say something like, "you poor thing," and make me feel worse. He just nodded, waiting for me to say something.

"I wrote a poem about it," I finally answered. "I can bring it in next time if you want to see it." In it, I had compared my life to a puzzle with one piece permanently missing.

"Yes," he said, smiling. "I'd like that."

I also began to meet once a week with a tutor so I could learn to decode the mysterious script of the ancient Jewish people. It took a lot of practice, but after a few months, I mastered the alphabet enough to read. I liked being able to run my finger, right to left, along the text. I never learned what the words meant, but their harsh "ch" and "ot" sounded strong and emphatic.

The rabbi titled my Bat Mitzvah service "Can I Go with You? A Dialogue with the Still, Small Voice of Loneliness." On its cover, I drew a picture of a girl sitting under a tree, all alone. "The Glass Prison," the silent meditation I wrote, captured all of my angst at the time: "I feel like I'm locked in a glass prison. Strangers look in, I look out. No communication is made whatsoever through the wall I wear. There is a key to unlock my captive spirit somewhere. I long to feel your love and gather in your kindness. No one has found me yet. So alone, I am a prisoner of my own mind."

The service ended with a more uplifting quote from Clark E. Moustakas: "Let there be loneliness, for where there is loneliness there is also sensitivity, and where there is sensitivity, there is awareness and recognition and promise."

As the only Jewish girl at Hill, I didn't feel comfortable throwing a big party afterwards. Billy, Adam, and some of the other Jewish boys I knew in school did have Bar Mitzvah receptions and dances at Richmond's hotels. They generally invited girls they knew from their synagogues, leaving me out. I planned a simple service and a reception afterwards. I invited about a dozen of my friends from school. My extended family—both grandmothers, my aunt, my cousins—and family friends also attended.

As I stood to recite my Torah portion about God answering a cry in the wilderness, my voice was strong. The rabbi stood behind me, ready to prompt me if I lost my place, but I didn't. I was staring down my loneliness in front of the whole congregation, and I wasn't flinching. I felt powerful. My call to the pulpit cemented the Jewish identity I had previously wanted to shrug off. After the final prayer, I stepped down, exhilarated. For once, Mom was beaming. I was less lonely because I felt like I finally belonged somewhere.

The Liberals

I envied my cousin Naomi, who had continued her education in the model public schools her parents had started. She attended Bellevue, a racially mixed middle school. It was in Church Hill, one of Richmond's oldest neighborhoods, not far from the site of the old Chimborazo Confederate war hospital, which had become a national park. Naomi called her teachers by their first names and wrote science papers about mysterious topics like hemoglobin. I visited Bellevue one day when I had a day off from my school. Everyone, black and white, seemed completely engaged in the classroom activities. In creative writing class, one girl wrote a poem about how the school bus looked like a monster in the morning, but the red lights looked like cherries by the end of the day. I thought it was fun and wished I could go to a school like that. But my mother still thought the model schools were too unstructured and wouldn't teach the fundamentals.

Despite our initial dislike of each other, Naomi and I had grown to be friends. She wore Earth shoes, carried a woven Mexican handbag, and pinned her frizzy, brown curls into a bun at the nape of her neck. She was shorter and more petite than I. Nobody could believe we were cousins because we looked so different from one another. Her house was always fun to visit. It was much larger and brighter than mine, with colorful Marimekko shades in the bedrooms and mod furniture, including a round, lacquered table with Le Corbusier chairs in the den. The full-time housekeeper, a sturdy, black woman they called Nora, set up sewing and cooking projects for us. The Zellers had all the modern conveniences my mother refused to buy—a dishwasher, a disposal, a side-by-side refrigerator with an ice maker, a stereo. There were pet rats, tropical fish, two dogs, and a cat.

Naomi had more of a political conscience than I did. On the stereo in her den, she played stacks of records by Joan Baez, Tom Lehrer, and Arlo Guthrie. She could chant slogans that made fun of Vice President Spiro T. Agnew, who resigned in disgrace 1973, and President Richard Nixon, who followed by resigning in 1974. I remember the evening that I watched President Nixon resign. I was at summer camp, where the girls in my group were given special permission to come to the director's house to watch Nixon's speech. Nixon was no more than three inches tall on TV. I felt like his scandal had nothing to do with my life. I already felt unpatriotic, disconnected from the national government. All around me, I saw people disobeying laws about school attendance, putting their own agenda ahead of what was supposed to be the public good.

One night, while my family and the Zellers ate dinner together at an Italian restaurant, Naomi and I went into the parking lot because we were bored.

"See that?" said Naomi, pointing to red schoolhouse stickers on the bumpers of on a few cars in the lot. "Those are bad. Those people don't believe in the public schools."

"So that's what the stickers mean," I said. "I never knew that."

"Let's rip them off," she said, looking around to make sure no one was coming.

Crouching, we set to work on the first car, a blue Plymouth. The sticker came off quickly and I crumpled up and threw it in the weeds at the corner of the lot.

"Bravo!" said Naomi. "Let's get another." We managed to yank off three other stickers before the parents came out to tell us it was time to go. I was nervous that someone would catch us and didn't want to be yelled at, but nobody noticed. Our petty protest made Naomi and me both feel smug.

What's ironic is that the following year Naomi went to St. Catherine's, Richmond's long-established, snobbiest Episcopal school. Larry and Phyllis had grown disillusioned with the model schools for the very reason my mother had identified from the beginning: the loose structure often left educational gaps. They wanted to give Naomi what they thought would be the best college preparation possible. Like many liberals, their political beliefs could not override their concerns about the success of their own children.

I couldn't believe Naomi was willing to sacrifice her cool, artsy crowd at the model schools for a bunch of girls who referred to Jews as "Hebrews." It was a tough adjustment for Naomi, who came to define herself as a rebel. She refused to bow her head in chapel, where attendance was required. She also flouted the dress code until one of the administrators called Phyllis to ask that Naomi start wearing a bra to school.

Naomi's brother, Sammy, went to St. Christopher's, the boys' school that was paired with St. Catherine's. When someone drew a swastika on his car windshield, Larry and Phyllis sent him to boarding school. Naomi also ended up at an elite boarding school in New England. In some ways, their abandonment of the public schools was a success. Both Naomi and Sammy were accepted to the nation's top colleges. Yet neither got to finish the multiracial educational experiment their parents had worked so hard to create.

Legacy of Defeat

The Zellers were the financially successful cousins. The Great Depression haunted the rest of my mother's extended family the way The War Between the States haunted other Richmond families. The fallen aristocracy and the legacy of ruin were similar.

From the turn of the century to the 1930s, my great-grandfather had built a successful real estate business in Richmond. He was at one time one of the city's largest landowners. Grandpa Henry went into business with him in the 1920s. In her diary, my great-grandmother wrote "DOOM" in black ink above the announcement of a foreclosure on the family properties in 1932. This put an end to the family real estate business after thirty nine years. Right next to the announcement, she placed Reinhold Niebuhr's Serenity Prayer: "Give me the serenity to accept what cannot be changed. Give me the courage to change what can be changed. The wisdom to know one from the other."

My great-grandfather died within months of the foreclosure. Whether it was a suicide depends on which family member I ask. Everyone agrees that the disappointment and shame of losing everything he had spent a lifetime building was simply too much for him to bear.

I imagine the gloom that descended after the foreclosures and my great-grandfather's death. Grandpa Henry, the courtly gentleman who cultivated his father's friends and glad-handed his way through real estate deals, would have been hunched in one of the living room chairs, fretting about the bills and how he could avoid losing face among his friends. Grandma Hanni would have hovered solicitously around him, asking whether he wanted ice water or fresh tobacco for his pipe. She learned to economize, shopping for bargain dresses instead of picking the first one off the rack. She kept using the silver flatware and trays that had been wedding presents, but she put her fine jewelry in the safe deposit box. She said she didn't think it would look right on her ten-dollar dresses.

My mother must have skulked at the margins, sensing the darkness but not knowing how to name it. She was shooed out to play with other children in the neighborhood, told not to complain or make too many demands. When she was nine years old, the bank foreclosed on the house in which she lived, with its view of paddleboats on the lake in Byrd Park and acres of parkland across the street. Grandpa Henry's brother, Ed, rescued them by finding the two-family house where he and Grandma Hanni still lived when I moved to Richmond.

My grandfather, who had no college education, took a job in the blending room at the Philip Morris tobacco plant. Apparently, he was so depressed by this job that most nights he came home and went right to bed. To help make ends meet, my grandmother, who could play the piano, took a job as music teacher at a nursery school. She had graduated Phi Beta Kappa from Barnard College, but she never expected to end up with a career as a nursery school teacher and director.

My mother seemed to inherit the family's sense of defeat. My father's death wounded her so deeply she stopped wanting to make our home a cozy place. Although she earned a salary from teaching and my father had left life insurance, she never felt comfortable spending any money. She was stuck in the mentality that had helped her family endure the Great Depression. My mother probably never realized how cruel her frugality seemed to my sister and me. She kept the heat at sixty-two degrees, day and night, and told us to put on extra sweaters if we said we were cold. We had to turn the oven off during the last five minutes of cooking so we could use the retained heat. She stalked behind us when we left a room, turning off the lights with a loud click, berating us for wasting electricity. If we spent more than ten minutes in the shower, she banged on the bathroom door and loudly reminded, "Have you seen the size of my water bill lately?" Though our house came with central air-conditioning, she never let us use it. On humid, ninety-degree summer nights, she gave me a flimsy electric fan to balance on a chair at the foot of my bed. Its anemic breeze gave me little relief; my pillow was soaked with sweat.

My mother saved every plastic bag, twist tie, paper bag, cottage cheese container, ketchup pack, rubber band, cookie tin, and jelly jar that crossed her threshold. She filled the cabinets with items on sale—cookies, canned soup, peanut butter, crackers. Then she kept them until they were stale. Hoarding probably made her feel more secure.

My sister was willing to argue with her, something that exhausted both of them. I learned to ask for as little as possible, to expect little physical care from her. Silence was safer at home, just as it was at school.

Silence was also the way my mother coped with her overwhelming grief about the abrupt loss of my father. I had only seen her crying once, and that was by accident.

Right after my father's funeral in West Virginia, we drove to a cousin's house for deli platters. It had turned unseasonably warm, and my wool jumper was itchy. Some Silverstein cousins tried to interest me in a game of Parcheesi, but I didn't feel like playing.

I wandered upstairs, trying to find something to do. I peeked through a half-closed door of a bedroom and saw a jumble of coats on the bed. I was about to walk in when I saw Mom standing in the shadows near the closet. Grandma Hanni was patting Mom's shoulders. Mom's hair was loose from its bobby pin, her nose and eyes bright red. Here, she was letting out all the sobs that she so carefully hid from Suzanne and me. Stunned, I crept away, sure that she would be angry with me if she knew I had spied on her.

My own tears roiled up inside me. If I did cry right there, who would comfort me? Not my mother, who would scold me for being where I did not belong. Not my sister, who had earlier dared me not to cry at the funeral. We kept looking at each other during the service to see who would lose the dare, but neither of us cried. The dim hallway gave me no answers. I took a deep breath, tiptoed back downstairs, and slid onto the edge of the brown leather couch where my cousins watched TV.

In Richmond, we continued to hide our tears from each other—if we allowed ourselves to cry at all. I imagine my mother alone in her bedroom after my sister and I had fallen asleep. She kept her door half-open to alert her to any emergencies in the middle of the night. The bedside lamp, still in its cellophane wrapper, was turned off. The magazine was set down, still folded open, on the floor next to her. Across the room was my father's old bed, piled with her letters, magazines, and newspaper clippings.

There was nothing more to push away the grief that had been floating in front of her all day, as she went to work, bought groceries at the Safeway, made dinner, held forth about the day's news at the dinner table, soaped and rinsed the dishes, set them in the drain board. Nothing to do but blunder into its disorienting, gray swirl, let her shoulders sag, let the tears leak out. Afterwards, she must have balled a tissue up in her hand and tuned her transistor radio to the late-night news program that might distract her enough to get her through the night.

When I woke in the morning, my mother was always dressed and downstairs, the *Richmond Times-Dispatch* spread across the yellow-and-white Formica table and the WRVA morning newscast with Alden Aaroe crackling from the radio. This was the mother I was allowed to see—the one with her hair combed, her blouse buttoned to the top, her tea made, and her grief tightly packaged and held somewhere I couldn't reach it.

I got used to using the word "deceased" when filling out forms asking for my father's name. I never got used to telling people I had no father at home. I knew no one else who had lost a parent. I found a way to get it over with as quickly as possible: the flat statement, "He died when I was seven." I felt embarrassed to be so different and I didn't want the stunned look, the hastily mumbled, "Oh, I'm sorry."

I felt more numb than bereft. Had I grown up in Charleston, among my father's family and his boyhood friends, I might have gotten more of a sense of him. As it was, he was forever preserved in the photo that my mother kept on her bureau, behind the bottle of Chanel No. 5 he had given her as an anniversary present. In his face, I saw the ghostly image of my own nose and lips. He looked so solemn in his suit, tie, and glasses, not the way I remembered him running along behind my two-wheeler.

It was painful to think about him because I had so little information. What would he say to me? Would he approve of the girl I was growing into? Would he even recognize me? My light brown hair came from him, but I was about the same size and shape as my mother. Did I inherit any of his personality traits? I sometimes felt like I was the child of my mother and a stranger. Thinking about him was like looking into a mirror in the dark. I knew a face was there, but I couldn't see it.

Holding the photo and pressing my lips to the glass, I tried to feel any signal that he might be trying to send me from the hillside in Charleston where he was buried. I tried a few times, but came up cold and had to wipe the frame on my sleeve so my mother wouldn't notice any smears I had made.

What would he say to my sister, who prodded, challenged, and argued constantly with my mother? The tension between them crackled through the living room like downed wires. I holed up in my room beneath a poster of a bare, ice-crusted tree with the saying, "In the midst of winter, I found inside me an invincible summer." I spun the dial of my transistor radio, the staticky blare preferable to the loud voices downstairs. My fear that Suzanne would turn her monstrous rage against me kept me behind my bedroom door.

What would he say to my mother? Would he see her floundering beneath her tight exterior? Would he tell her to step back and lighten up on the petty household rules, let my sister find her own way? Would he urge her to go on sending me to the school where I had become invisible, my sense of self vaporized?

It was easy to imagine him as the savior of our family life because there was no one else to step into the breach.

No Yearbooks, No Good-Byes

My middle-school years ended not with a graduation ceremony or a yearbook—our school didn't offer either—but with a threat. It started during our eighth-grade field trip to Hershey, Pennsylvania. I sat in our chartered bus with Liz and another white friend, Janine, as the driver blared Marvin Gaye, Curtis Mayfield, and other soul music. The volume gave me a headache after an hour. The ride took four. Janine, who was tough and wiry and cursed more than any of my other friends, walked up the aisle and asked the driver if he could turn it down. He shook his head and said, "Uh-uh. It's the only way I'll get through this drive."

One of my black classmates had brought as a chaperone Miss Coombs, an aunt who seemed to be in her early twenties. When the bus stopped in Hershey, I immediately stood up and tried to get off.

"Sit down," Miss Coombs said. She was about my height, but her girth and her haughty posture made her seem taller. The smoothness of her brown cheeks made her eyes pop out.

"Why?" I asked, impatient after the long ride. She marched down the aisle and pushed my shoulder so hard that I fell back into my seat.

"Because I told you so. Don't you give me any lip," she said.

When we were finally allowed to leave the bus, we divided into small groups. I went off with Janine and Liz and to ride the roller coaster and see the Hershey's Kiss–making machine. Miss Coombs glared at me when I returned that evening.

In the days that followed, word spread among the black kids that Miss Coombs wanted to beat me up on the last day of school. Miss Coombs's niece gave me dirty looks whenever I passed her. I was stopped so often—at my locker, in homeroom, on my way from one class to another—that I began to take the threat seriously. At both Binford and Hill, the prospect of an interracial fight always loomed over us as white students. It was fueled by the very real hostility in the halls and bathrooms, as well the myth dating back to slavery that black people are violent and uncontrollable. I never witnessed an interracial fight, though I heard plenty of rumblings from blacks and whites, boys and girls, about someone's "ass getting kicked." Miss Coombs was the first to specifically target me. I was horrified that she would carry my one petty defiance so far, and that she would bother to threaten a girl half her age.

About a week before the end of school, I told Mom I didn't want to go to school on the last day.

"You are required to be in school every day," she said.

"I don't want to go. It's a waste of time. Nothing happens."

I didn't want to tell Mom the real reason, that I was frightened. I thought she would make me go anyway, or embarrass me by calling the principal. This could only backfire into a more severe beating, I was sure.

On the last day of eighth grade, I simply refused to go to school, no matter what my mother said. It was the first time I had played hooky. Liz stayed home, too, in a gesture of solidarity that I appreciate to this day. We went back and forth between our basements, lying low. I felt I had no choice. Miss Coombs and her threats, idle or real, ruined whatever sense of closure I might have felt from my last day of middle school. I never even said good-bye to my teachers or my classmates.

Singing "Dixie"

Every summer from 1971 through 1974, my mother sent me away to Camp Mountain Laurel in the mountains of North Carolina, near Asheville. When she was growing up, she had gone up north to a camp in Maine every summer. She believed that camp was just as much a part of my basic education as the public schools.

I bunked with five other girls in a cement-floored cabin with screens for windows. Many of them were the descendants of Confederate leaders in Atlanta, Savannah, New Orleans, and other southern cities. Some were the daughters and granddaughters of governors and senators. Everyone at the camp was white. None seemed to be affected by desegregation, even if they lived in cities like New Orleans or Little Rock. They went to suburban or private schools, dismissing their public schools as terrible.

I didn't know how to explain my school in Richmond. If I just talked about my teachers and my friends without mentioning the reason I rode the school bus, or the white table in the cafeteria, or the fact that I couldn't even think of dating most of the boys I knew from my classes, then I could pretend I was like everyone else.

It was hard enough being Jewish at Mountain Laurel. There were only a dozen Jews out of about 250 campers and counselors. All of us had to go to chapel every Sunday, dressed in white. The chapel was in the woods next to the Green River, with pews made out of split logs and a wooden cross made from logs nailed together. We had to sing "The Church in Wildwood" as we walked in and "Onward, Christian Soldiers" as we walked out. I was surprised the first time I heard the Lord's Prayer, the initial "Our Father" followed by the rush of mumbling and bowed heads. My desire to look like everyone else won out over the pang that I was being a traitor to my own religion. I learned every word, though I never recited too loudly from beneath my bowed head.

One day in the dining hall, I was interrupted by a windy "A-wayyyy, a-wayyyy" from the other side of the room. I looked up to see a group of older girls standing up, singing "Dixie." They raised their fists each time they came around to singing, "In Dixieland, I'll take my stand to live and die in Dixie!" In order to fit in, I stood up, sang along, and even raised my fist at the right time. After that, I regularly joined in the singing several times each week at meals or in the morning assembly.

I split myself in two, the way my mother did between being a daughter of the South and a liberal teacher. When I was at camp, I raised my fist and sang the Rebel anthem. When I was at school, I would never admit to even knowing the words to "Dixie," much less to having sung it all summer. I kept my head down, fearful of being punched for saying or doing the wrong thing. I couldn't fully identify with either place. I didn't feel that "Dixie" was a proud part of my heritage to claim, no matter how loudly I learned to sing. Then again, I didn't take pride in being one of the few white girls at school, either.

The safest thing to do at camp was distract myself with the new things to learn: how to build a campfire and start it with a single match, how to sit in a canoe, how to rig a sailboat. I liked backpacking and camping best of all. What I lacked in size compared to the older teenage girls, I learned to make up for in endurance.

It rained the first time I went on an overnight hike to a wilderness area called Cantrell Creek. I tramped along a dirt road, my boots soaked, my shoulder-length hair plastered to my head. I had never thought of the true meaning of shelter before. That night, we stayed at a cabin and dried our socks by the fire. The next day, we hiked along the creek and pitched tents for the night. I woke up and looked out the tent flap at the maple leaves overhead and the mist coming off the ground. I smelled the damp rhododendron. I didn't care that my fingernails were still dirty and that all I had to wear for the day's hike was a muddy pair of shorts. In the woods, I had finally found a place where it didn't matter what flag I sewed onto my jacket, or whether I was supposed to recite the Lord's Prayer.

The disconnect between my life in Richmond and the life of other white girls my age became even more apparent the Christmas in 1973 when I went to visit Jan Eisner, a friend from camp. The Eisners lived in Clayton, one of the St. Louis suburbs. I was thirteen years old and flew by myself on the airplane. Their pale, brick house had a garage with a door that opened by remote control, something I had only seen once or twice before. Dr. Eisner, dressed in tennis clothes from a game at his club, came out, shook my hand, and carried my suitcase inside.

The next day, Mrs. Eisner took us inside the St. Louis arch. The elevator that took us to the observation deck kept twisting sideways as it climbed the curves. When Jan began to look pale, her mother patted her knee.

"This ride is always hard on her," she confided. I liked being with Mrs. Eisner, who seemed so approachable and relaxed compared to my mother.

At the top of the arch, I looked down at the Mississippi River and imagined where Huckleberry Finn had paddled his raft. I liked the wide, flat sweep of the city. In the winter, it looked tidy and efficient, unlike Richmond, which seemed clogged with foliage, humidity, and statues of Confederate heroes that turned green in the rain.

That night, Jan and I played pinball at the machine in the Eisners' basement. We could take as many turns as we wanted without having to plug in quarters. I asked Jan about her school. Here's how I remember the conversation:

"It's kind of normal, I guess," said Jan. "You know. There are jocks, freaks, cool people, brains, the usual."

"Are there any black people?" I asked.

Jan wrinkled up her face to think about that. "Well, there's Sam and his sister, Denise. There's a boy in my brother's class, I think. That's about everyone."

I laughed.

"Why is that funny?" said Jan. "They're nice. Sam is the star of our basketball team."

"So you don't have busing," I said.

"Well, some of us take a bus to school."

"That's not what I mean."

"Oh, like busing where they throw rocks at the black kids going for integration? That kind?"

"Yeah, that kind."

"No, we don't have that."

"You're lucky. We do."

"Yeah, but do you have to be bused? I thought it was just for black kids."

I was starting to get annoyed because she really didn't see what I was talking about. We had never had this kind of conversation during the summer, because there had been too much else going on at camp. Who wanted to talk about school when we could be swinging on a rope and jumping into the lake?

"It's not." I said, irritated. "Do you know what it's like to be practically the only white person at school?"

"No," she said, and was quiet for a minute while she thought about it. "But why do you have to do it? Why don't your parents — I mean why doesn't your mom — send you to private school?"

"Well, it's kind of expensive. Besides, if nobody white goes to the public schools, how will they be integrated?" I said, repeating my mother's arguments.

Jan shrugged and went back to her pinball game. "I don't know," she said.

I leaned back into the couch and pulled my knees up to my chin. Jan was so naïve. I looked up at the ceiling, with its Tiffany-style Coca-Cola lamp, and wondered what it would be like to live here. To have a father, a little brother, and a garage door that opened at the push of a button. To have a mother who patted my knee. To go to school where the worst thing to worry about was whether you were a "freak" or a "brain."

I was so jealous of Jan that I wanted to walk out and tell Mrs. Eisner to take me back to the airport. But Jan had been my friend all summer. She still was my friend. But I wished she could understand what I was going through.

"You don't get it, do you?" I said, about to cry.

She turned around and looked at me, hands still on the flippers of the pinball machine.

"Don't get all sore," she said. "Who wants to think about school? It's vacation! Let's have fun while you're here. C'mon! Let's go upstairs and see if we can make one of Mom's recipes for a citrus face mask. It's supposed to be good for your pores."

I followed her up into the kitchen, taking the stairs two at a time.

At the end of my final summer at Camp Mountain Laurel, my counselor wrote my mother a letter saying that I was "too Jewish" to fit in with the girls in my cabin and suggested I not come back. Even then, I would have described myself as standoffish, but to attribute that to religious differences showed my counselor's biases and misinterpretation of the situation. I preferred to keep quiet as the girls whined about how much they hated camp, or made fun of the "jigaboos" they knew back home. I spent most of my time on canoe trips, or playing the guitar with Jan, who lived in another cabin and who also happened to be Jewish. I was outraged that my counselor had trampled on all that I had appreciated about camp. The wilderness had been my tonic each year, a chance to lose myself in the sweep of mountains and the fog that nestled in their valleys. In this setting, I could feel like a human being, not a Jew, or a white girl, or the daughter of a dead man. Now it was time to find another destination.

The Open High School

When I started high school in 1974 right after my final summer at camp, I always carried a book ready to shield the front of my face. I was all brains and skittishness. Not knowing what to do with my woman's body, I hid it under jeans and a baggy smock. I let my hair grow long, thick, and ropy. I had reached what would be my adult height, a mere five feet two inches. My weight was what doctors would call average, but it was still higher than I wanted it to be.

I had chosen to enroll in the Open High School, an educational experiment run by the Richmond public schools, the high school version of the model schools started by the Zellers. It is ironic that I ended up at the Open High while the Zeller children went to boarding school. There were 160 students in all four grades, about 60 percent black and 40 percent white. The academic mix ranged from would-be dropouts to geniuses who would go on to earn Ph.D.s. Anyone who lived in the city of Richmond was eligible to go.

My mother, despite her misgivings about the model schools, was willing to let me apply to the Open High instead of continuing on to Thomas Jefferson, the traditional high school she and my sister had both attended. She knew I hated eighth grade and wanted to try something new. Because I had thrived in the English independent study class at the Richmond Humanities Center, she thought I was finally mature enough for the less structured Open High.

By going to the Open High, I left Liz and whatever friends I had managed to make in middle school. Our group had been dwindling each year, anyway. Of eleven white girls from our cafeteria table at Binford, only two of us continued in the Richmond public schools through high school. By the end of eighth grade, I felt we were a ragtag bunch who stuck together just because we were white. Had we met in any other situation, most of us would never have become friends.

The direction that the Richmond public schools would take was decided in 1973, when the U.S. Supreme Court ruled on a proposal to consolidate Richmond's city and suburban school systems.

The black plaintiffs envisioned one giant school district that would mix the white students from the suburbs with the black students from the city. At this time, the Richmond public schools were 70 percent black. The schools in Henrico and Chesterfield counties, Richmond's nearest suburbs, were more than 90 percent white. A giant school district would have given each school a more even racial mix. U.S. District Court judge Merhige ruled in favor of this plan in 1972.

Consolidation, as the plan became known, outraged the white, suburban families who would be affected by it. Many had moved to the suburbs to escape busing in the first place. In 1972, a motorcade of 3,261 cars drove to Washington, D.C., to protest. The *Richmond Times-Dispatch* called Merhige's decision "appalling," further editorializing: "U.S. District Judge Robert R. Merhige, Jr. is more interested in manipulating human attitudes than in promoting excellent public education. This he showed by warmly endorsing . . . the pernicious gibberish of those social engineers who argue, in effect, that a school system's primary function is to promote racial togetherness, not to give children the best possible academic education." In the spring of 1973, the U.S. Supreme Court overturned Merhige's ruling. Justice Lewis Powell, former chairman of the Richmond School Board, recused himself from this decision.

The Court's decision, which meant that the Richmond schools would not see a fresh influx of white students, set the stage for what was already happening during my school years: overall enrollment was declining and the ratio of black students was increasing. In fall of 1970, the year desegregation started, there were 47,988 students in the Richmond public schools, of which 64 percent were black. When I graduated from high school in 1978, there were only 35,412 students, and 82 percent were black.

While the courts were wrangling over the school consolidation plan, the Open High quietly opened as a Richmond public school in 1972. Instead of operating in a traditional school building, it rented headquarters on the second floor of a downtown Richmond office building. The principal styled his gray-streaked hair in an Afro, and he wore a sports shirt instead of a jacket and tie. Everyone called him by his first name, Al. We also called our teachers by their first names. The main room was a lounge where everyone sipped sodas and smoked cigarettes between classes. Some played chess or ping pong. Others draped themselves over the frayed sofas and chatted. Everyone looked artsy and cool.

The Open High was structured like a college. Classes met all over Richmond, at all times of the day and night. We were given free tickets to use the Richmond city buses for transportation. We could take whatever classes we wanted, as long as we earned the right number of credits for graduation. There were about six full-time staff teachers (also known as "resource people") but also dozens of volunteer teachers—potters who taught ceramics, graduate students who taught history or English, bankers who taught finance. We could also take tuition-free classes at Virginia Commonwealth University (VCU), though only for high school credit.

During my first week at Open High, when I was paired up for a trust exercise with a junior nicknamed Zippo, I realized that the racial atmosphere would be much better than at my previous schools. Zippo was black and gangly. He bounced when he walked, and he wore nerdy, black-framed glasses. I wondered how I would be able to spend an hour with him. We set off down Franklin Street to the park outside of the Virginia State Capitol, which had been off limits to blacks (except gardeners) just ten years before. I'm sure a few heads turned when Zippo and I walked through the iron fence posts together and settled onto the grass near a magnolia tree. Foremost in my mind was completing the exercise and returning to school, not making a racial statement.

I still have the exercise, printed in purple mimeograph ink. The directions read: "The main purpose is to cross cultures so that we might better understand each other as individuals. Some of the basic areas that might help us achieve this understanding are: self-disclosure (telling about ourselves), self-awareness (seeing ourselves), risk taking, trust, acceptance, and clear communication and feedback on what you've learned."

In one section, I had to list derogatory terms about black people (nigger, spade, coon, boy, Uncle Tom). In another, I had to list derogatory terms about my own ethnicity (dirty Jew, whitey, big-nose, schmuck). I listed Martin Luther King, Frederick Douglass, and

Harriet Tubman as three influential black people; former presidents Kennedy, Lincoln, and Johnson as influential white people.

In describing my most awkward racial encounter, I wrote, "I walked on an all-black bus and everyone stared at me funny." This had happened one day at Binford; I had accidentally stepped onto the school bus headed to the black Gilpin Court housing project. My choice of encounter surprises me now, but I think I must have been trying to stick with something fairly safe. It was probably the first time I had talked directly to a black boy about racial issues. If I had known him better, I might have talked about how ashamed I felt the day I wore the Confederate flag on my jacket, or how much I hated orchestra and wanted to join the band.

When it was Zippo's turn to talk, I learned of his devotion to Jesus and the Catholic Church, and his interest in guitar playing. He was already an old hand at the Open High. I wrote, "You are not as weird as you think you are" and "You are not afraid to be yourself" as his strengths.

It was a relief to see mixed-race groups in the school lounge. The Open High seemed to be one of the few places in Richmond where black and white students got along fairly well. The do-your-own-thing atmosphere kept racial problems to a minimum. Living on the fringe was not only tolerated, but celebrated. There were teenage mothers who sometimes brought their babies to class with them, openly gay and lesbian students, punk rockers, LSD freaks, and a sixteen-year-old who lived with her college-age boyfriend instead of her parents.

Still, I couldn't find the right place for myself. I was supposed to check in each day with Lynne, my "family head," the equivalent of a homeroom teacher. Her office overlooked Franklin Street and the parking deck where two Open High students were once arrested for smoking pot in the stairwell. Unless she was conducting a class or holding a meeting, students lounged on the windowsills and on her desk. If I stepped inside, everyone seemed to stare at me, then return to their conversations as if I wasn't there. The best I could usually do was join in a chorus of "Lola" or "Be True to Your School" when Zippo broke out his guitar. Lynne, fresh out of teacher's college, with the look and figure of a Barbie doll, seemed a bit bemused by the freewheeling school she had landed in. Still, she was the only one who encouraged me to talk. She also encouraged me to stay at the Open High when I wanted to go back to TJ, where I thought I would feel more comfortable.

I wondered what I was doing wrong. My Osh Kosh overalls were as fashionably tattered as the next person's. I could confidently make my way around the city on the buses and my bike. But I carried thick scars from my past years of busing. Gone was my confidence in making conversation and being friendly to anyone, of any race. I became known as a bookworm and a snob who never talked to anyone—which only made me withdraw more.

I never saw Liz anymore because my schedule was so different from hers. She was also becoming more interested in finding a boyfriend and less interested in our old adventures, like sneaking cigarettes behind the weeds at the Exxon station or pouring puddles of nail polish on the sidewalk and lighting them on fire. One afternoon, on my way home from the Patterson Avenue city bus, I walked past her yard and saw her jumping on the trampoline, her long, auburn hair flying up. Having slimmed down as she grew taller, she now looked more like a model than a tough tomboy. With her were two or three girls I didn't recognize. She waved. I stood on the sidewalk, my knapsack sagging under the weight of my books, watching her fling her arms out with each bounce. I was heading home, and she was aloft, her new friends clustered around to spot her. With sadness, I waved back and continued walking.

I Surrender!

I began spending the time between classes at the Richmond Public Library, just across the street from Open High. I started out sitting in the cushioned yellow chairs of the carpeted reading room, but I was often interrupted by snoring homeless men. I then began sitting at a table near the stacks of nonfiction. I spent hours there, doing my homework or reading books by Nathaniel Benchley, Sylvia Plath, and Vladimir Nabokov. The books were safe, didn't require anything of me.

I might have become a total recluse had I not started talking to Andrew Gordon, a boy who also spent a lot of time in the library. I met him the first week of school when I went to Capitol Square with Zippo. He was on the grass, his long legs sprawled in front of him, eating lunch with a group of other students. As he listened to the conversation, he bent his head to one side, his light brown curls brushing the top of his T-shirt, his brown eyes intent. I was so attracted to him, I gulped before I introduced myself and giggled after I said my name. I found out that he was also a freshman.

In the spring we took a history class together, taught by an earnest VCU graduate student who assigned us a college-level research paper, complete with footnotes and bibliography. One day, I unloaded my knapsack in my usual spot in the library, a table near the reading lounge, and started writing notes on an index card. A few minutes later, Andrew came over and sat down.

"Hi," Andrew whispered, clearing his throat. "What are you working on?"

"Hi," I whispered back, so we wouldn't make too much noise and be shushed. "I'm doing the student revolts in Paris in the 1960s."

We talked about our papers for a while. I watched the minute hand of the wall clock advancing from 3:10 to 3:25. It was time for me to pedal off to my French conversation class, but I decided to skip it. I thought this conversation was more valuable than one in French.

The librarians began to glare at us, so we walked outside. Andrew propped himself up on the rack where I had chained my bike. We kept talking, mostly about school. I wanted to keep talking forever, but I was starting to shiver. It was April, and the air cooled as soon as the sun cast long shadows across Franklin Street. Soon, it would be rush hour, a time I hated riding home. I would be squeezed to the margins of the street.

"I have to get going," I finally said. "I'll see you tomorrow."

The next day, he sat with me in the library instead of at his usual table. After that, we started making plans to meet each other.

Like me, Andrew had attended predominantly black middle schools. He told me how one day in gym class some black kids had ganged up on a white boy and thrown him into a dumpster. I was simultaneously amused and horrified by this story. Andrew seemed to get through his years in middle school the same way I did—by keeping to himself and reading as much as possible.

One warm afternoon in May, Andrew and I both decided to skip our classes. He needed to shoot a roll of film for his photography class. We headed south to the Robert E. Lee Bridge across the James River. We stopped at the War Memorial, but the setting was too somber for our exuberance. We continued to a construction site for the city's downtown expressway. He took photos of the bulldozer and the river, and one of me leaning against the bridge railing.

On the walk back, he grabbed me and pretended to throw me in the water. At first I struggled, and then I simply leaned back into his arms and said, "I surrender!" He didn't push me away. We stood like that for a minute, the traffic rushing north and south and the muddy James roaring underneath the bridge. I could feel the heat of his chest through his T-shirt, smell the soap on his skin. His chin tickled the top of my head. Slowly, I turned around and looked up at him. His face stood out against the downtown skyline—the gridded sides of City Hall, the cluster of towers at the Medical College of Virginia, the Central National Bank across from the Open High. I wanted to step anywhere into this panorama with him.

For the next three years, until we both were seventeen, I saw Andrew nearly every day. Having a boyfriend wasn't what I imagined from reading a magazine article about a boy who handed over his class ring and asked to go steady during a date at a drive-in movie.

It was meeting for lunch on the fire escape of an old brownstone building at VCU, sharing our sandwiches from home, or the subs we'd bought from the Up Top Sub Shop nearby. It was also trading paperback books; snorkeling side by side in the Florida Keys during a student science trip; following each other through the city on our bikes; lying in a deserted field late at night, the whirl of the Milky Way above us; and flinging away our clothes to face the heat and tumult of each other.

Buoyed by affection I had never felt from anyone else, I spent the weeks and months floating past the familiar landmarks of Richmond, casting away wads of pain and loneliness like unneeded ballast.

Belonging and Not Belonging

At the Open High School, I felt like I usually received a silent run-down when I tried to make conversation: "Who are you? Do you get high? Are you cool enough to talk to?" I felt far more welcome in the B'nai B'rith Youth Organization, a group for Jewish teens. At the first meeting I attended, I knew no one, but a lot of the girls made it a point to introduce themselves and ask me about myself.

When I joined B'nai B'rith, I instantly became part of all the things I had been missing: Saturday night parties, sleepovers at girls' houses, Wednesday pool or gym nights at the Jewish Center, and an instant dating network. There were even proms once a year, something too conventional for the Open High to sponsor. After so many years of social isolation at school, I had resigned myself to being invisible and unpopular. This group gave me a chance to make friends, go to movies and hockey games, and dance to Top 40 records — to feel normal at long last. Nobody else went to the Open High, and I don't remember any other girls who had been bused, but it didn't matter. Being Jewish knocked aside these potentially divisive differences.

As nice as it was to feel accepted, I still found myself living my life in different compartments. The B'nai B'rith world was a complete retreat from my school life. At VCU, where I took my English, history, and language classes, I was at least four years younger than most of the students, many of whom bragged of their sexual exploits in poetry workshops or swaggered around the campus carrying six-packs of beer. I did my work and kept quiet, afraid that talking too much would reveal my identity and make everyone label me "jailbait." When one professor announced to his entire class that the high-school student among them had earned the highest grade on the midterm, I leaned over, face burning. I was far from proud. I didn't want to seem like a child wonder. I certainly didn't feel like one. All I had done was study for the test. More than that, I didn't want to be "outed." I wanted to blend in as much there as I did anywhere.

The other thing that prevented me from fully identifying with B'nai B'rith was my relationship with Andrew, who wasn't Jewish. My mother never forbade me from dating non-Jews, though she did say she thought I would have more in common with Jewish boys. I was willing to tell my Jewish friends about Andrew and eventually to stop dating other people, but I couldn't bring him to any of the B'nai B'rith events. This was a Jewish-only group; outsiders were unwelcome, and I don't recall anyone breaking that rule. To mix non-Jews into the group would have ruined our sense of community, made us feel like we did anywhere else. Though Andrew didn't like being left out, I considered my B'nai B'rith membership too important to drop. I coped the same way I coped with singing "Dixie" at camp one month, then slinking through the halls at a desegregated school the next. I had one identity as an Open High student and Andrew's girlfriend; another as a Jewish teen; another as a high-school teenager trying to pass myself off as an ordinary college student. I felt like an actress with different lines to remember and recite at the appropriate times.

Driving Lessons

Because the Open High didn't offer a driver's education class, I signed up for a class at TJ in 1976, the year I turned sixteen. The atmosphere there felt like middle school all over again. Two boys were the only other white people in the class—and the only other students who would talk to me. We all trooped out to a trailer across the street from the school, shivering in the cold, spring air. The trailer housed a driving simulator, but we called it the "stimulator" as a joke. We had to watch films of someone driving a car and pretend to drive along at consoles built to look like dashboards. After a few weeks of that, we could take lessons in real cars.

The test-driving range at Parker Field, now the Arthur Ashe Center, was all the way north out The Boulevard, a traffic-choked street that passed the field where the minor-league Richmond Braves played. I hated riding my bike to the lessons, but it would have taken three bus transfers to get there. I arrived at the first lesson feeling sweaty and hassled.

Mrs. Jones, the TJ gym teacher, ran the driver's ed range. A thin black woman with a medium complexion and acne-scarred cheeks, she wore nylon sweat pants with matching jackets. She chewed mint gum and carried a clipboard. All of her assistants were black, mostly juniors and seniors at TJ who had recently gotten their licenses and needed an afternoon job.

During my first lesson, Mrs. Jones assigned me to LaVerne, a heavyset, dark-skinned girl who wore glasses with chunky gold frames. When she saw me, she looked irritated. I don't remember any other white students on the days that I took lessons.

"Get in," she said, motioning to the driver's seat. "Hands at 10 and 2," she ordered, meaning approximately where the numbers 10 and 2 on a clock would be. Then she climbed in next to me. The car had an extra brake on the passenger side, just in case the instructor needed to stop the car quickly.

"Now, go around the cones," she said, pointing to a series of orange cones that were set up in the gravel field. The idea was to steer around each cone without knocking it over.

I put the car, a four-door sedan, into drive and got around the first cone. The car's rear swiped the second one.

Boom! LaVerne jammed on the brake and glared at me. My body rocked back and forth in the aftershock.

"Get out and pick it up, girl. Anyone ever taught you how to steer?"

I climbed out, humiliated, picked up the cone, and climbed back in. LaVerne was yelling "Hey, girl! Whass up?" out the window to another instructor.

"OK, go," LaVerne said to me.

I made it to the end of the cones, but knocked one over on the way back.

LaVerne rolled her eyes, and said, "Why are you so dizzy?"

My head was spinning by the end of the lesson. It was getting dark and I had to pedal back home through the rush-hour cars whooshing past me.

The rest of the lessons went similarly. Even Mrs. Jones looked annoyed when she had to drive with me. Because she and her assistants had already pegged me as incompetent, I felt like I could do nothing right. I'm sure I was a bad driver to begin with—the same clumsiness that kept me out of the dance recital made my driving hesitant and erratic—but other teachers might have had more patience. No sooner did I start to relax than they jammed on the brakes to tell me my hands had slipped from the correct "10 and 2" position to "9 and 3," or that I was riding up on the car in front of me.

By the end of the driver's education class, my driving was worse than it had been when I started. I didn't even come close to passing the final test. I rode my bike home utterly dejected, convinced I would be stuck riding my yellow ten-speed forever. I felt singled out for scorn as the only white person taking lessons. The consequences were keeping me from a crucial rite of passage. Though my sixteenth birthday had come and gone, I was still asking for rides everywhere.

My mother, who sat on the passenger side of her car with rigid shoulders and stamped her foot on the floor every time she thought I should brake, was hardly suited to step in as my teacher. After sizing up the situation, she responded in a way that surprised me. She signed me up for private lessons with the American Automobile Association, and didn't complain much about paying for the lessons. Although she had supported the public schools in every other aspect of my education, even as the Richmond schools were gradually slipping in standardized test scores and other measures of quality, somehow, my learning to drive was important enough for her to turn to the private, and in this case, white, alternative. The AAA drivers—all white men over age thirty, as I recall—coached me through intersections, steered me past my misguided attempts at parallel parking, and helped me finally pass the driving test before I turned seventeen.

Preppie Envy

I had not realized how much I resented desegregation until the day during our junior year that Andrew and I went on a one-day student exchange to the Collegiate private school. The ride along River Road seemed to take forever. The school, surrounded by athletic fields, looked like it was in the English countryside. Inside, everyone was well scrubbed and white-skinned. The girls had to wear dresses or skirts. The operative dress code was preppie: Lilly Pulitzer prints, monogrammed sweaters, Blucher moccasins or duck-hunting shoes from L. L. Bean. I saw Annemarie, Billy, and a few other people from my past. They all seemed surprised to see me there.

In class, nobody smoked or called the teachers by their first names. Several teachers talked about the SAT, something most Open High teachers barely mentioned. At Collegiate, we trooped from one class to another. Bells rang. Students waved at each other as they passed in the halls. I walked around, amazed. This was the kind of high school I had read about in books. It was carpeted. The showers in the locker room worked. Nobody pushed each other in the halls. Everyone smiled. My occasional fantasy of being a girl in a perky ponytail with a mother who made waffles every morning came roaring back to life. I thought I had squashed it forever under the wheels of the city buses that took me to the Open High.

At that moment, I wanted to be at Collegiate more than anything. I wanted to look like everyone else. I wanted to go out for the track team. I wanted the guidance counselor to tell me that if I kept up the good work, I could get into Harvard. I wanted to drive to keg parties in my dad's car and giggle sheepishly the next day about being so wasted. I wanted things to be predictable, not a constant struggle to find my way around Richmond every semester and eke out a comfortable place for myself in the cigarette-hazed Open High lounge.

I hated myself for feeling this way.

That night, I started explaining all this to Andrew as we sat in his family's clunky Dodge Dart, on our way home after checking on a building he was renovating for an Open High class. I finally got too mad to talk anymore. I didn't want to start crying—not over some spoiled preppies! So I balled up my fists and held them against my chest.

"Clara," Andrew finally said, shaking me gently. "What do those preppies have that you want so badly?"

"It's . . . so . . . easy . . . for . . . them," I spat out.

Reiterating one of the main points my mother also made, he shook his head, and said, "They are deluded. They don't know the first thing about the real world. You have it all over them. You're more open-minded and you know it."

The value of being open-minded wasn't much consolation when I hated myself for having to survive too much of the real world. As a white person, I never expected to grow up in the midst of so much racial strife, to internalize it to the point where I felt like I was always on the outside of a beautiful paradise that I couldn't enter.

All this kept me quiet, but hardly at ease, as we drove back to my house, our hands clasped across the chasm of the front seat.

A Shell Tossed into the Ocean

One of the few times I felt connected to the Open High was during a camping trip in the spring of my senior year. I rode down to Virginia Beach in my teacher Lynne's yellow Chevy Vega, listening to the Paul McCartney and Wings tape loop around her eight-track player. Two classmates were crammed next to me in the backseat. My sleeping bag and knapsack containing a change of clothes and a toothbrush were piled in the trunk.

Two other classmates led the way on a motorcycle. The wind from the open windows—Lynne's car didn't have air-conditioning—plastered my hair to my cheeks. The music and rush of air were so loud I didn't have to try to make conversation.

We arrived at the campground before dark and set up a canvas army tent vast enough for our entire group of fifteen or so. We were about evenly split between girls and boys, black kids and white kids. For dinner, we ate pizza and Coke from the campground store. It seemed like the easiest thing in the world to be sitting between two black kids, passing around slices of pizza. After dark, we played cards by flashlight at a picnic table. Most of the other kids went into the tent to get high. I was the only student who stayed at the picnic table playing cards with the teachers.

Around midnight, we all laid out our sleeping bags in the tent. I slept in a T-shirt and shorts. I dozed for a few hours, then woke to the slap-slap-slap of the breeze blowing a metal zipper against the tent pole. I propped myself up on my elbows and looked around. Outside the tent flaps, I could tell the sky was just beginning to lighten. Lumpy sleeping bags surrounded me. I could make out Lynne's blonde ponytail in one corner, a boy's Afro in another. All around me, there was a mosaic of kinky and smooth hair. The air was filled with the whoosh and hiss of people breathing while they slept.

I crawled out of my sleeping bag, pulled a sweatshirt out of my knapsack, and tiptoed out of the tent. The wind brought the scent of salt. Barefoot, I picked my way across the road, then down a trail lined with dune grass. The ocean was on the other side of a small rise of sand. Across the damp sand, I could see the stringy tracks of fiddler crabs leading down to the water. I walked down to the surf and let it splash across my ankles. Then I sat on the dry sand, watching pink etch the clouds.

I drew my knees up to my chest, shivering, and was surprised to find myself remembering my father. When I was about six, my family and I had rented a cottage at Virginia Beach. Dad had taken me on an early morning walk, leading me by the hand across the dunes. For most of my life, I had pushed such memories out of my daily thoughts. I didn't want to get stuck watching them play like an old movie, everyone's movements too jerky and the soundtrack too slow. I closed my eyes and tried to let something clear come back.

I felt his rough palm covering mine. Then I let myself imagine him alive, walking up to the campground, peering into the tent, and turning back to me, smiling. One of his fondest dreams was for me to live with people of all races. This is why he bought a house in Hyde Park. This is why he stationed himself in the middle of our Red Rover games in the backyard, a black child holding one of his hands, a white child holding the other. He wanted to make links so strong nothing could break through.

I was just beginning to realize that Dad had given me a gift by raising me in Hyde Park. My years in that neighborhood showed me that racial harmony is possible. Dad's vision is what sustained me through being spit on and the rumors that Miss Coombs wanted to beat me up. I had already seen another way. I didn't hate the people who treated me badly because they were black; I hated them because they were mean. In the few short years that he was part of my life, Dad had managed to guide me toward the tent where my classmates of both races now peacefully slept.

I picked up a shell and tossed it into the Atlantic Ocean. "I dedicate this moment to Joseph Lee Silverstein Jr.," I told him, the power of speaking his full name setting off the tears I had been holding back for years. I sobbed until my shoulders were sore. Then, feeling better, I rinsed my face with ocean water, turned away, and walked back to the campsite for breakfast.

The Education Mom

Because my mother left early for work, I usually didn't see her until dinnertime, when she would push through the front door, a book bag filled with teaching magazines in one hand, a swim bag for her daily laps at the Jewish Community Center in the other. She kept her hair cropped close to her head, strands of gray now weaving through the dark roots. Her shoes were always flat and sensible, her skirts plain, her twenty-year-old cardigans buttoned, her face unadorned by makeup. She had little interest in dating, although she would sometimes go out if someone fixed her up. She usually reported that the man was a "sad sack" or not right for her.

After my sister left for college in 1975 — never to return home for more than a brief visit — my mother yelled less, but continued her constant vigilance about turning off the lights and turning down the heat.

My mother was at her best when it came to education. We ate dinner together in the dining room, whichever newspaper article she wanted to discuss with me folded on the table next to her, a dictionary on the sideboard in case there were any words we wanted to check. It was my chance to tell her my opinion of Watergate, women's lib, drugs, or anything timely.

Sitting at the head of the table with a plate of carrot and celery sticks and a platter of pan-fried minute steak in front of her, she listened. She probed. She told me what she had read in *Future Shock* or *Passages*. It was my private tutorial in current events.

Best of all, she kept an open mind. She didn't seem upset when I told her that most of the kids at the Open High bragged about smoking pot. She knew what pot was, though she had never tried it and said she never wanted to.

"It doesn't interest me," she said, laughing. "I don't need something artificial to have a good time. But that's what kids do today. I know you're going to try it." I thought this was a surprisingly hip comment for someone over thirty.

Getting high was the least of my concerns. I was too serious and too much of an outsider at Open High to sit around the back stairwell toking and giggling with the potheads. The odor from this stairwell was a constant embarrassment to the Chamber of Commerce next door. A teacher sometimes disciplined us at the school's weekly "town meeting," announcing with a snicker that the Chamber was complaining again and it was time for everyone to find another place to get high.

If conversation was the setting in which my mother felt comfortable, physical care was another story. I was basically on my own with a wretched case of mononucleosis toward the end of my senior year in 1978. I had to make the doctor's appointment where I received my diagnosis, ride my bike to the office, and then ride home again before I could collapse in bed. For several days, I did nothing more than watch the light thicken into morning, flare against the venetian blinds, then fade again. My limbs sagged, my throat throbbed, and my head felt like it was stuffed with cotton. Reading made me dizzy. My mother was out all day, stopping by just long enough to bring me soup or give me Tylenol and then leave again.

In this condition, I had no escape from the pain of my breakup with Andrew a few weeks earlier.

"I've been thinking," he said one morning when he stopped by my house after one of his classes. "I really ought to get into better shape. Open High doesn't have any teams. I want to start jogging in the mornings. Why don't you try it?"

I stared at him.

"I ride my bike everywhere, why do I need to start jogging?" I asked. I had tried jogging a few times, but I usually ended up gasping and doubled over with a stitch in my side.

"I just have to start doing something different," he said, fiddling with my bike's brake cable. Then he looked at me and said, "What I mean is, we have to cool it for a while."

Logically, breaking up made sense. I wanted to leave Virginia for college and he didn't. He was getting restless for all the teenage stuff that we had missed by spending so much time together—keg parties, driving late and fast in a carload of kids, dating different people. The relationship was beginning to implode from its sheer intensity.

We had begun bickering over trivial things, like which movie to see, or what kind of birthday presents we bought each other.

The day he asked to "cool it," I was still wearing the shirt I had slept in. I suddenly realized how disheveled and exposed I looked. I could have listed ten reasons why it was for the best, but I still felt like I had been abruptly dunked underwater and had to fight my way back to the surface to take a breath. In the days that followed, I had to break the daily habit of him. All the mundane things I used to tell him piled up like sticks, crunched by his heel as he walked past me at school with a gruff "Hi."

After I had been bedridden for a week, my mother stepped in and made me get out of bed. She held my arm as we went downstairs and supported me as we walked slowly down the front walk, up to the corner, and back again.

She kept trying to cheer me up as I recovered my strength. One night, as I tried to catch up on my calculus homework, she came into my room and asked if I'd like to see the Indian musician Ravi Shankar perform the next night. She stood beside my chair, absently brushing the eraser crumbs from the edge of my desk.

"I think you'll like it. I went to a concert of his in Chicago, right after your father died. It was one of the first things I did that made me feel like I would be OK again," she said, with uncharacteristic candor.

My mother was trying to help me get out of my funk about breaking up with Andrew in the best way that she knew how, by tamping it down, staying busy with other things, getting out of the house.

I nodded and said, "Thanks."

Sure enough, the concert was an exotic, if short-lived, tonic.

It might have been around this time that my mother told me she had burned my father's love letters to her. I remember her words landing with a dull thud: "They were nobody's business." She had destroyed everything—their pet names for each other, their plans, their passions. I was left to forever swirl through the smoke, choking, fanning the air for clues about their relationship.

Racial Differences Still Evident

When I was a freshman at the Open High, I started as a correspondent for the weekly "Young Virginians" page of the *Richmond News Leader*, the city's afternoon newspaper. The first time I walked into the newsroom, phones were ringing, typewriters were clattering as reporters filed their stories, and editors were yelling questions across the room. The energy in the room hummed through me, making me feel more alert. Richmond's news nexus seemed like an exciting place. I didn't care if the editorial writers at the paper constantly railed against desegregation. I wanted to be sitting at one of those desks, a telephone cradled on my shoulder, scrawling in a notebook and saying, "Now, how do you spell that?" into the phone. By dropping off one of my stories at the *News Leader*'s downtown office, I had stumbled into my future career.

The Open High had no clubs or sports to cover, unless you counted the occasional Ultimate Frisbee game, so I wrote about offbeat classes like cosmology or the ecology of the Outer Banks. Everyone at school started calling me Lois Lane. If they saw me coming with my notebook out, they sometimes teased, "Oh, no!" But they usually wanted to see their names in print. I liked it because when I interviewed them, I could take control of the conversation. I didn't have to try to stumble through small talk. I could get right to the point: "What do you think is a status symbol?" "Why do you go steady in high school?" "What is appealing about Reverend Sun Myung Moon?"

My reporting got me inside the first black person's home I visited in Richmond. A group of Open High students helped turn the late Maggie L. Walker's home into a National Historic Site. Walker had lived in a two-story brick house on East Leigh Street in Jackson Ward, one of Richmond's oldest black neighborhoods. She was the first woman in the United States to start a bank. The house was still filled with the fringed lampshades and family photos that Mrs. Walker kept until her death in 1934. Some of the students sat cross-legged on the couch in the parlor and pretended to sip tea. We all laughed at their exaggerated manners.

I wished I were visiting a home where a black family was still living, but I didn't know any black people well enough to be invited. The atmosphere at the Open High wasn't to blame for that. I just found it easier to spend my time roaming the city for my classes or my newspaper stories, keeping to myself, observing and taking notes, hiding my true self because I didn't want to be rejected anymore.

I wrote a lot of my stories at my father's old Royal manual typewriter, which I set up on a rickety typing table in the corner of the den. I liked feeling this connection to him. He had been the editor of his high school and college newspapers, using the same typewriter to do some of his writing. I thought that if he could see me bent over the keyboard, trying to pull together a story from the notebooks and papers next to me, he would be proud.

In June of 1978, right before I graduated, I wrote one of my last articles for the *Richmond News Leader*'s "Young Virginians" page. Beneath the headline, "School Racial Differences Still Evident," I considered busing's legacy in Richmond. By then, the Richmond public schools were 82 percent black and 18 percent white. At that time, Richmond had so few Hispanic and Asian residents that they didn't register in the statistics. I interviewed students and adults of both races, including Richard C. Hunter, Richmond's first black superintendent of schools. After the article was published, he wrote me a personal note thanking me and wishing me success in my future writing projects.

In researching that article, I finally got to ask all the questions that had been bugging me for years: Did everyone think the educational standards had fallen? Why did black and white students sit on opposite sides of the cafeteria? Did anyone socialize with mixed-race groups after school? Did anyone think integration was working?

There were no easy answers. Most people said that they stuck with members of their own race, in school and afterwards, because they felt more comfortable with them. People also lived far away from each other and couldn't always drive to get together outside of school. Some black students admitted that they tested white teachers to see whether the teachers were willing to work with black people. A white girl talked about having to prove her athletic ability to her black schoolmates because "I had to show them they can't push me around." White people who started in public school and then switched to private school said they liked having more in common with the other students but thought the atmosphere made them "less open-minded."

I caught up with Phil Robinson, who had been the lone black student in my class in elementary school. He had continued on to Maggie Walker High School, one of Richmond's black schools before desegregation, where he was back in the racial majority. He had a unique perspective: "The schools are dominated by blacks, but the world is dominated by whites. People get misled if they are in the majority for a short time. The world is going to throw things in their faces, and it is going to be hard to adjust."

Most people, black and white, said that they considered integration a long and slow process. The most realistic, but hopeful, answer came from a white student who told me, "When two different groups are thrown into a school, tension naturally results. But gradually people get to know each other and work together."

My social circle illustrated how few white people were willing to do this kind of work. All of my friends from elementary and middle school had ended up in private school or in the suburbs — even Liz, one of the last holdouts, who left TJ during her junior year. In my graduating class at the Open High, there was only one boy who had attended my elementary school. This, in brief, was white flight.

I do think that education suffered because the school system believed itself to be in decline. I wonder if Richmonders perceived the system this way, because education was always considered inferior at mostly black schools, even after desegregation was supposed to equalize everything. Expectations were low, even for an honors student like me. In middle school, we were supposed to turn in our homework and follow along in class, but few teachers talked about college. People labeled the whites in the honors classes as the smart kids. The black kids in the same classes were often scorned as nerds and Oreos, or they were viewed as exceptional.

At the Open High, it was not assumed that everyone would go to college. Those who did generally went to schools in Virginia or elsewhere in the South. I don't remember the school guidance counselor helping me choose where to apply to school, or even telling me how to sign up for the SAT. Few people at my school had heard of Wesleyan University in Connecticut, the college I decided to attend. It had no prestige in Richmond, though elsewhere it was considered one of the top colleges in the country, part of the so-called Little Three that also included Amherst and Williams. A lot of people asked, "What's wrong with the schools in Virginia?" and told me, "You'll freeze to death up there with all those Yankees." Undeterred and defiant, I ended up being the only member of my graduating class to go to college in New England.

Was This a Good School?

I was leaning against a pillow on the floor of my freshman dorm at Wesleyan University in 1979, listening to Pink Floyd's *Dark Side of the Moon*, when several people decided to start passing around their high-school yearbooks. I expected to laugh at everyone's goofy senior pictures, but instead I found myself squirming. Next to the chronicles from the Madeira School, Concord Academy, Loomis-Chaffee, and Beverly Hills High School, my Open High yearbook looked like the Third World. My ragtag classmates played chess and Ping Pong in the school lounge. Teenage mothers snuggled their babies in class. Wannabe punk rockers posed behind the trash cans in the school alley. There were black faces on almost every page.

It looked nothing like the green, manicured world in everyone else's yearbook, a world that I claimed not to want but hated not being able to have.

"Wow!" said the self-proclaimed Grateful Dead Head who lived down the hall. "Where was this?"

"Let me see," said a student from L.A., who already knew the make and model of the cars belonging to everyone in our dorm. He frowned and said, "Was this a good school?"

I didn't know how to answer that. By going to Wesleyan, I had walked into an elite club of students groomed for success. There was a small percentage of nonwhite students at Wesleyan; ironically, many had gone to prep schools and fit in better than I did. I felt like I was there by fluke, like everyone else was more sophisticated, more self-assured—in a word, superior. My high school wasn't anything remotely "good." Some of my graduating class didn't go to college at all, and those who did never even considered schools like Wesleyan. I answered with a shrug, then choked down my shame with a hit from the joint that was going around. That year, I was finally experimenting with the marijuana I had so long resisted, holding in the smoke until my chest hurt.

A paper I wrote about some of busing's cruel realities received this response in red ink: "Basically, you have mis-identified the enemy. Blacks (and the nasty things they can do to whites) are only a symptom of the real problem, U.S. capitalism, which ripped Africans from their families and tribes, and brought them here as slaves, and has kept them in a horrible, inferior condition ever since."

I could see a lot of truth in this leftist interpretation, but it was irrelevant to the point I was trying to make. I wasn't prepared to turn my experience into a political discussion, so I stuffed the paper into a folder and picked a completely different topic for my next assignment. Why did I feel so ashamed? Wesleyan was the land of "Question Authority" buttons and "Divest from South Africa" rallies. My participation in a movement for social justice should have made me a hero. Instead, nobody knew what to make of me. The most searing lesson—what it felt like to be a minority, even though I'm white—seemed to have no value. I made people feel uncomfortable because I had not followed the familiar and understandable trajectory to success. I reminded them that they had not participated in desegregation, perhaps because they were never ordered to, perhaps because their parents prevented it.

I choked down my shame all year as I learned to wear sweat pants to class, play the metallophones and gongs of the Indonesian gamelan, and write papers about Aristotle. Late at night, tired of trying to keep pace with everyone, I wandered through the tunnels under the dorms, trying to decipher some profound truth from the graffiti. The philosophy ranged from "A man without a god is like a fish without a bicycle" to support for Frank Zappa's ambition to move to Montana and become a dental floss tycoon.

I spackled over my Richmond past so thickly that by the time I graduated, I didn't even have a southern accent anymore. I stuffed all of it into a dark place inside me because I didn't want to answer any questions about it, didn't want to reveal how different I was from everyone around me, didn't want to be pushed away.

Only in my African American history classes did my desegregation experience seem useful. After a lot of reading, I began to see Malcolm X as visionary instead of a militant kook. I listened to stacks of blues records, heard the suffering tempered by humor, learned how to play along with a harmonica. The black students I met in these classes kept to themselves afterwards, preferring their community at the Malcolm X House to the sea of white students that surrounded them. Nobody ever asked why I was so interested in African American history, and I never tried to explain, thereby missing a chance for a discussion that probably could have educated all of us.

My Father's Words

The closest I ever came to hearing my father talk to me as one adult to another was the day after I had graduated from Wesleyan, when I found his old diaries in my mother's basement. Here was the account of his U.S. Navy service when he was twenty. He sailed to the Philippines in 1946, right after the war had ended. It wasn't at all like the soldiers' letters I had read in my history classes, filled with jokes and fond memories of high-school buddies back home. My father wrote about the day he saw a Filipino boy picking through the trash for an apple, and then went to the Army Officers' Club "replete with a swimming pool, an eight-piece orchestra, and a bar well stocked with whiskey and beer of several brands." He continued, "It occurs to me, if the Army and Navy spent more money on rehabilitation of the Filipinos and less on recreation facilities for officers, they would be losing fewer Jeeps and black market goods. The comparison of the hedonistic Officers' Club and the child with the apples makes me ashamed to wear the uniform of the U.S. Navy."

In another entry, he mused, "Sometimes, in thinking over American history as it is told in textbooks, I get the impression that there is a serious discrepancy in the character of our people between former times and now. In the old days, say the books, Americans were generous and they fought for freedom and justice and the rights of man. The crooks and carpetbaggers and government-grafters never lasted very long, for the righteous wrath of the American people always drove them under. Nowadays, it seems to me that almost every group is interested in its own benefit first and the good of the whole second."

I sat down at my desk—the same desk that he had used in Chicago—and began to copy sections of the journal. I didn't want to lose this contact with him. All morning, I put his words into my own handwriting, the felt-tipped pen gliding across the pages of my spiral notebook, the tears occasionally splashing down and smearing the ink. It was my father who had taught me to form the cursive letters in my name, copying and recopying C-L-A-R-A so I could trace the lines. Now, I was tracing his words once again.

In the diary, and in his other papers, his fatherly advice was all there. His opinion of marriage: "A marriage founded on true understanding is far more likely to succeed than one founded on animal attraction." His prime objective in life: "To live an ethical life, to follow the golden rule and help others whenever possible." His reason for becoming a lawyer: "I have been guided somewhat by my desire to change the status quo, and to obtain more justice and an equal opportunity for all."

When my mother came home later that day, tossing her canvas work bag by the front door, I told her what I had found in the basement. She smiled.

"Good for you," she said. "I always meant to tell you to go and look down there one day."

"He was so idealistic!" I said. "I never knew that."

"Yes, he was," she said, closing her eyes and exhaling sharply. "He was always getting disillusioned with everything because of that. Nobody was ever ethical enough for him. He always took that so hard."

I nodded, waiting for her to go on. She turned her back to me and started dusting the cloisonné box on the mantel with the sleeve of her sweater.

"You know," she said, "in some ways, I think he was too good for this world."

"No, I don't know," I answered. "There's a lot I don't know."

Years later, when I was back in Boston sorting through a box of papers my mother had given me, I found my father's 1961 diary. I was born just three months before he began keeping the diary. His name was stamped in gold letters on the red cover. When I read it, I sat at the bottom of the basement stairs. Squeals and thuds from the cartoon my children were watching on TV drifted down from the living room.

"I am going to try to keep more of a diary this year," my father wrote on January 1. Loops of blue ink filled in the details. He was teaching law at the University of Pittsburgh, interviewing judges from around the country for an Institute of Judicial Administration

138

study, and writing articles about bankruptcy and other legal topics. He took my sister to nursery school on a sled and played the clarinet for her after supper. My mother organized dinner parties and went to teas and Pittsburgh Symphony concerts. They quarreled about what they could afford, my mother always saying no at first, then "coming around."

He was way ahead of his time about racial equality. On January 10, he wrote, "Two Negro students admitted to University of Georgia. Hurrah!" On January 12: "The Negro students at Georgia were suspended because the white students rioted. I would have suspended the whites." The next day, by coincidence, he was a guest speaker giving a talk entitled "Religion, Law, and the Public Schools" at the Homewood Elementary School's PTA meeting. "The school is almost all Negro. Very clean. I stayed to tea and cookies afterwards."

His premonition of his untimely death made me shudder as I kept turning pages in the dim light. He often felt "faint" and "short of breath." A friend's death got this reflection: "Al died last night of a sudden heart attack. He was 52. I wonder if I will reach that age or older." On his thirty-fifth birthday, he wrote, "I don't feel any older, but my responsibilities are certainly increasing. I've got to take good care of myself so I'll be here when the girls grow up." A few days later, he wrote, "The death of Patrice Lumumba at age 35, plus my recent birthday, makes me pause and reflect on what I will amount to, what contribution I will make. I think that improvement of the administration of justice is a worthwhile and attainable objective."

Worthwhile and attainable. How lofty and intellectual he sounded! He died a hero to me, his noble goals preserved for me to read forty years later. My mother had to go on, inspired by his vision, suffering from his loss. She stayed true to his ideals about integration, sending me to be bused without hesitation. But she had to do it without his leadership and inspiring rhetoric. He might have been the missing link in my experience, the parent who lovingly stroked my face—the face that became numb, a mask over the shame that roiled inside me.

Would my father still have sounded so lofty as he watched his daughter turn into a silent white girl—one who felt as invisible as Ralph Ellison? Where was the premonition that everything about desegregation would spin out of control, like a school bus hitting a patch of ice?

Had he lived, he might have inspired policymakers. He had published one book about defending the poor; he planned to write other books. His legal aid work was written up by *Time* magazine. He wanted to be a judge. Could he have been the leader who came up with a workable integration plan? Or would he have been eternally frustrated by the gap between his goals and the grind of living them?

I clapped the covers of the diary together, covered my face with my hands, and cried about the injustice of it all. My children, unaware, kept watching cartoons.

I Am Lee's Daughter

I was just a few years shy of forty-two, the age of my father when he died, the weekend I flew to West Virginia for the 125th anniversary of Temple Israel. My father had worshipped at this synagogue, along with the rest of the Silverstein family. At the hotel, I put in my contact lenses and blinked at myself in the mirror. As my face swam into focus, I examined myself for evidence of my father's genes. My hair color, now streaked with gray, was the most obvious link. I also saw a ghostly image of my father's face in the shape of my eyebrows and the contour of my cheekbones.

After the Shabbat service, I sipped a cup of punch and scanned the room for cousins, some of whom I hadn't seen since my grandmother Bertie's funeral ten years earlier. My father's sister, Aunt Betty, prompted me when I couldn't remember someone's name.

A stooped man with gray hair came up and gently touched my elbow. I turned and he introduced himself. It wasn't a name I recognized.

"I'm Lee's daughter," I said, surprised at how unfamiliar, yet how appropriate, that sounded.

"I heard you were here," he said. "I knew your father. Very well, in fact. We were in school together."

"What do you remember?" I asked, eager to add to my aunt's collection of stories about how she and my father played tag on the lawn of the West Virginia State Capitol and rummaged through the trash there to find postage stamps for their collections.

"He was so serious," my father's friend said. "He had an amazing memory. It was photographic, really. His mind was like a steel trap. Did you know his nickname was 'The Professor'?"

"Well, I know my mother used to call him 'The Absent-Minded Professor' because he tripped over his feet when he was busy thinking about something else," I said.

"That sounds like Lee!"

We smiled at each other. "It's so nice that you came," he said, shaking my hand before he walked away.

My aunt drove my mother and me to the cemetery, up a winding road to a hillside overlooking the Kanawah River and the buildings that dotted the mountainsides. Fall had splashed the oak and redbud trees. It was only the third time I had seen my father's grave. Its headstone is a simple granite rectangle, with his name carved in capital letters. When she dies, my mother wants to be buried next to him.

We silently emerged from the car, and each walked in separate directions. I watched my mother and aunt, the backs of their dark coats receding, and wished they would turn around. Wouldn't it be nice to embrace each other, to say the Kaddish, to place flowers on the grave? Their slow footsteps crunched the gravel, and I realized that this is the only way they know how to grieve: alone, silently. Letting Jewish tradition take over, I picked up three stones—one for my father's headstone, one for my grandmother, and one for Joe, the grandfather I never knew. After watching me, my mother silently did the same.

Then I pulled out my notebook and played the role I know all too well, the one I am trained to do, the one that can mask my feelings: journalist. I quizzed my aunt about our ancestors, taking notes about each one. Then I took photos of their headstones.

Later, I changed into jeans, zipped my jacket against the October chill, and left the hotel. I wandered through the food court of the mall across the street, then went outside. It was getting dark. I walked down Capitol Street, which Aunt Betty said used to be the center of town before the mall came. I tried to imagine the neighborhood as my father might have seen it one afternoon from his two-wheeler: his father's law office around the corner; cars with isinglass windows; girls in cardigans and blouses with Peter Pan collars, boys in crew cuts; the twang of the West Virginia accent in every conversation; mountains looming over everything; the Kanawah River slicing through, lights from the opposite shore faceting its surface.

I tried to imagine growing up here, and what it might be like to drop by my father's office and ask him for a quarter so I could get a milkshake at the Blossom Dairy. To pedal home and find my mother's cheesecake cooling on the lattice-covered back porch. To see mountains from my bedroom window. To be surrounded by family, the trajectory for my future predictable and secure.

I shivered and pulled my jacket tighter, hurrying back to the hotel because I didn't want to be out alone after dark.

Splinters of Glass

My husband and I look as white as anyone else and blend right into the liberal Boston suburb where we moved to raise our children. I realize that we're here because we have the money and the skin color to fit in, and at times I do feel guilty about it. But I also admit that I want to give my children the chance for an easier life than mine.

No matter how I look or where I move, there is no escape from my past. My experiences are lodged inside me like splinters of glass. In a recurring nightmare, I am alone, wandering the neighborhood behind Binford Middle School because I have missed the afternoon bus home. A group of black boys ride past on their bicycles. One spits at me and laughs when the spit splatters at my feet and I recoil. I hoist my knapsack, filled with the schoolwork that I am supposed to be doing at my house. People on the street corner glare at me as I walk past. I duck into a store, hoping to buy a soda or a candy bar, anything that will be familiar. When I reach into my purse, I find no money, hold up my empty hand, and the clerk says, "Get gone!" I stumble out, and walk in circles, dark and hostile faces riding by in cars, watching from porches, in a ring around me.

In another recurring nightmare, I am driving, either alone or with my children in the backseat. I lose my way and end up in a black neighborhood. It's like walking through the corridors at school again, everyone glaring at me. I decide to pull over and ask a man for directions. I roll down the window, and he laughs at me. I wait for him to answer me, but he keeps laughing. I roll up the window and pull away, my foot shaking as it presses the accelerator. I circle around and around, with no foreseeable escape.

After one of these nightmares, I wake up, still lost. It takes a few minutes for the gauzy darkness in my bedroom to resolve itself into the familiar bureau and chairs. I wander down the hall to my children's rooms, carefully navigating in the night-light's glow. Their faces are slack with sleep.

The fear and rejection stay with me more than the moments of grace, like secretly holding hands with Walter or playing Christmas carols in the halls. An adult who lived in my situation, with the abrupt changes, the departure of so many friends, and the division of the community, might have been able to step back, talk about the lessons learned and the greater good. As a child, I took all the pain inside me and felt like a failure for not being able to understand it all and find a place for myself.

The adults who could have helped steer me through the tumult failed. The principal cancelled social events, the teachers were too wary to discuss race, the black parents focused on the struggles of their own children, and the white parents pulled their kids out of the schools. My mother believed in desegregation but was oblivious to its emotional consequences for me. She still says, "Everyone has to suffer when they're trying to change things. The world is not made for just white people." She's right, but that doesn't take into account how I experienced the suffering, and how she and other adults might have helped me cope.

My experience never changed the Richmond schools. Judge Merhige ended busing in 1986 because by then, the schools were 87 percent black. What my experience did was change my perspective about race. The most powerful lessons that I learned as a white girl in predominantly black schools aren't those that my mother or the policymakers might have predicted. The expected answer is, "I learned to get along with all kinds of people" and "I learned to value diversity." At school, I didn't learn those things. The divisions and suspicions were just too deep for me to make a close black friend, much less date the black boy I liked. I came out despairing that the schools, as I experienced them, would never lead the way for any of us to make lifelong changes in how we interacted as two different racial groups, each with a different history and perception of America.

What I did learn, at least initially, is that being in the vanguard of social change can be a lonely, not a heroic, place for a child. My education put me so far out of the mainstream that I ended up having little in common with the vast majority of white students my age. My role in integrating the schools, and later my attendance at the Open High, prevented me from following the familiar script of playing school sports or watching games, achieving a class rank, and attending school with the same group from kindergarten through high school.

I was lost.

I learned to discredit the American history told in textbooks — as my father had, but for a slightly different reason. The version I read dwelled too much on the triumph of colonial heroes over Indian savages and British tyrants; the pride of Richmond as the birthplace of U.S. Presidents and capital of the tragically doomed Confederacy; and the Manifest Destiny of westward expansion. This version glorified democracy as the world's greatest system of government, while ignoring racism. The schools, in their ineptitude, left it to the black students to teach me that not everyone sees the Confederate flag as a symbol of pride, and that the legacy of slavery is brutal.

I acted as a parent, not as a survivor of school desegregation, when I signed up for an antiracism meeting at a housing project in Roxbury, a minority neighborhood in Boston. The black parents at this meeting sent their children to suburban schools through a voluntary busing program called METCO. I listened as they explained how their children were invited to play at suburban homes, but the white parents hardly ever wanted to drive into Roxbury because, they said, it was too dangerous. The elementary school children seemed to accept each other, but there was usually a change in middle school, when interracial dating became a possibility. At that point, the black students tended to stick close together, not wanting to test the boundaries by socializing too much with their white classmates.

This sounded achingly familiar — some thirty years after I was bused. I realized that in order to do anything with my experiences, to truly become my father's daughter, I had to start speaking.

I raised my hand. My voice faltered, then tumbled out. "I, well, I'm not sure how people are going to take this, but . . . I think I understand why black children want to sit at their own table in the school cafeteria."

The room went silent and everyone stared at me. I considered stopping. Who really wanted to hear this white lady, anyway? But I forced myself to continue.

"I was a white child bused to a black school during desegregation in the South, and we had a white table in our lunchroom. It has to do with feeling like an outsider . . ."

When I finished, people of both races nodded.

My cheeks burned. This was the first time I had ever told a group of black adults about my experience of busing. The old fears and misunderstandings made me anticipate the worst—that someone black would jump up and say, "Shut up, honky! What do you know?" But this time everyone listened respectfully.

Only when I attended meetings in Richmond to commemorate the fiftieth anniversary of the *Brown v. Board of Education* decision was I finally able to claim some pride in having stayed in the public schools when so many other white students had fled. My skin color no longer felt like a liability, even though I was one of the few white people in the room. My experience was completely different from the experiences of black people, but we shared the goal of educational equality. In the end, I believe the legacy I carry forward is positive, even though the *Brown* decision often pushed me into confusing and painful territory. My experiences enlarged my view of the world. As I confront my past and whatever prejudices still linger, I want to join an ongoing conversation about how to improve race relations, even if I don't always know what to say or what can be done.

If I could relive my childhood, I would go back into a racially mixed school, but one that magically avoids the cruelty and misunderstanding, the hurt feelings and missed connections because of race. There's nothing wrong with Martin Luther King's dream that "children will one day live in a nation where they will not be judged by the color of their skin but by the content of their character." What went wrong was the execution of it, the unwillingness of policymakers and families to confront the history and consequences of oppression. Children don't care about social change. They have no perspective on history. They just want to make friends. In the words of Dr. King, they want "to join hands" and "walk together as sisters and brothers"—with anyone who accepts them.

Some of the old, throat-choking fear wells up as I step out of the car in front of Binford Middle School and help my son and daughter out of the backseat. I haven't walked into the building since leaving in 1973. I wrap my arms around my children's shoulders to steady myself. Up the stairs we go, all together. In the hall outside the office, I point out the drawing of the school that Sandra and I found in the orchestra room's storage closet and gave to the principal to have framed. I am amazed to find it still on display. The students frolicking on the front lawn of their whites-only school make it as much of an anachronism as ever.

The children and I tread up the ramps and down the stairs. The cool, high-ceilinged halls with polished floors have changed little. The playground is still pure asphalt, and the Main Street traffic still whizzes by outside the fence. The downstairs girls' bathroom still has the slatted wooden doors on the toilet stalls, and the same concrete floors and sallow light. Ghosts of the hostile girls flit by, but the room is deserted between classes. I lift my arms and start whirling around, clapping, and shouting "Wooo! Wooo!"

Martha turns away from the mirror, astonished. "What are you doing, Mommy?" she asks.

"I can spin around in here! Nobody's here to stop me!" I shout giddily.

The bell rings, and students come pouring out of the classrooms. The hall echoes with their voices. Jordan and Martha come out into the hall and start spinning the wooden tops we bought at the Valentine Richmond History Center, shrieking playfully as the students sidestep them. With their white skin, they stand out in the crowd the way I used to.

As my children and I walk out Binford's front door, I prepare them for the story that I one day want to tell them.

"You know, a long time ago, it was against the law for black children and white children to go to the same schools," I say.

"Why?" asks Martha, tugging my hand, eager to go to Byrd Park for the slush cone and a ride in the paddle boats that I have promised.

"Well, that's a long story. But I went to this school to try to change all that," I say.

On the way to the park, I drive south across Cary Street, through the neighborhood where my black classmates used to live, through ordinary-looking streets and houses that I have never seen before.